The Breath of God

Ron Crawford

Published by Pneumatikos Publishing
P.O. Box 593531
Dallas, TX 75359
E-Mail: info@pneumatikos.com
www.pneumatikos.com

First printing, September, 2005
Second printing, September 2013

ISBN-13: 978-1482701142

Cover Art Work by Fabian Arroyo

Unless otherwise noted, scripture quotations are from the HOLY BIBLE, Authorized King James Version.

Table of Contents

Introduction

Someone once said "man is a spirit being, enduring a temporary human experience." It is somewhat difficult to attribute initial authorship to this Biblically accurate observation, but whoever said it first is deserving of commendation. Mankind is a spirit being, as each human has been endowed with the image of God. We simply live in the midst of this human frame.

There is generally much confusion about what it actually means to be a spiritual person. What does the word "spirit" mean, anyway? For many people, there is a strange reaction within whenever anyone talks about "spirit." These folk are either frightened by the discussion; or they gullibly pursue any and all contentions; or they are locked into a sense of false doctrine formed throughout their life, absolutely meaningless from a scriptural perspective.

To say a person is "spirit-filled" is another area thoroughly misinterpreted while at the same time being adamantly grasped as a pillar of faith and identity. What does it mean to be spirit filled? What about the concept of being created in the image of God? Does this imply we are spiritually inclined, or does it simply mean we have been formed in such a way as to pattern the Most High?

While this book does not promise to answer all conjecture concerning the Spirit, there will be an attempt to dispel some measure of confusion by reason of the simple truth of the Word of God. The contention of this writing will be that the Spirit of God intends mankind to commune with the Heavenly Father. This is, in essence, the chief goal of God for His creation.

We must bear in mind whenever we say "spirit" in conjunction with either the Old or New Testaments, we could easily be saying "breath" or "wind." When the peculiarly translated "ghost" is interjected into the conversation, it could also very easily be translated as wind or breath.

In order to understand what God is saying to us regarding this subject, we must dispel superstition and fanciful notions in order to grasp the heart of God. So much of what we think we know hinders the progression of truth into our hearts. While we should firmly hold the traditional things that yield life and health, we should be willing to observe the ideal of God sharing a new thing with us from His Word. This should especially be the case when such insights involve the identity of His presence and nature.

The Breath of Life

The Hebrew word translated as the breath of human life is *n'shammah*. According to the Biblical narrative, when God created Adam, He "puffed" this breath into man to initiate life.

> *Genesis 2:7 And the Lord God formed man of the dust of the ground, and breathed (naphach – puff) into his nostrils the breath (n'shammah) of life; and man became a living soul.*

Throughout the earth, this life-giving dimension is seen. Over and over again during the many centuries man has walked the earth, this is the way life begins. No country or continent is exempt. No people group can say they are formed differently

2

from anyone else. This is the rule of life, as God has granted life-giving respiration to all.

Isaiah 42:5 Thus saith God the Lord, he that created the heavens, and stretched them out; he that spread forth the earth, and that which cometh out of it; he that giveth breath (n'shammah) unto the people upon it, and spirit (ruwach) to them that walk therein:

The breath of the Almighty gives life to mankind, but the act of breathing is not sufficient in itself to bring life to man. Without the *ruwach* of God, or the person of God Himself, there would be no life. Job said the person of God is the prevailing factor of life. God Himself willed life to mankind, and respiration could only have meaning because of divine intention.

Job 33:4 The Spirit (ruwach) of God hath made me, and the breath (n'shammah) of the Almighty hath given me life.

It is important for man to realize that breathing, in itself, is not life. Breathing is merely existence. To really live, humanity must embrace the spark of life inherent within each of us. Job said this dimension of the life of God is within each of us, and respiration is given so we might probe and understand the Almighty.

Job 32:8 But there is a spirit (ruwach) in man: and the inspiration (n'shammah) of the Almighty giveth them understanding.

In the Image of God

Perhaps it would be wise to discuss what it means whenever we say Adam was created in the image of God, after His

3

likeness. The Hebrew word *tselem* is translated as image and possesses a meaning of an illusion, a shadow or a resemblance. Image does not imply spirit or wind, in this instance. The Word rendered as likeness is the Hebrew *d'muwth*, meaning a model.

> *Genesis 1:26-27 And God said, Let us make man in our image (tselem), after our likeness (d'muwth): and let them have dominion over the fish of the sea, and over the fowl of the air, and over the cattle, and over all the earth, and over every creeping thing that creepeth upon the earth.* [27] *So God created man in his own image (tselem), in the image (tselem) of God created he him; male and female created he them.*

What can it possibly mean that men and women are created in the shadow or resemblance of God? In my thinking, these colorful descriptives speak of mystery and intrigue. A shadow drives someone to an investigation of the source of light causing the shadow. This would also imply the shadow as being a reflection of what is standing in the light. Both of these imply emulation and potential. Fundamentally, whatever mankind achieves will be judged by how we reflect the image of God through our identity in the face of His light.

God made mankind with the potential to represent and be like Him. There is also the curiosity within every person that longs to pursue Him. The inherent drive of mankind to know and to learn is inevitably a result of this shadow as it searches for meaning. We must be careful to seek the light of the one true God, and not settle for the light which is really darkness.

> *Matthew 6:23 But if thine eye be evil, thy whole body shall be full of darkness. If therefore the light that is in thee be darkness, how great is that darkness!*

4

Breath is a Candle

The breath within the lungs was given so mankind might gain an understanding of God. The Book of Proverbs declares the breath of man is actually the candle of God.

Proverbs 20:27 The spirit (n'shammah) of man is the candle of the Lord, searching all the inward parts of the belly.

What is the significance of the candle of the Lord? Could it mean God allows man to see Him in a subtle way, not with a brilliant beacon but with a restrained but discernible glow? The candle could be indicative of gentle reminders from God, speaking of His presence to each person.

A candle produces alluring shadows, and is in itself a romantic icon. Whenever a candle is present, the light cast by it possesses great intrigue and attraction. Picture a candle sitting upon a table, or a candle upon the nightstand in a darkened room. These are visual images that provoke great imagery within our minds. Something about a candle implies the desire to pursue what has been illuminated, as well as what is just beyond the reach of its scope of luminance. Things look different by candle light than by any other light source. Perhaps it is due to the fiery source of the light itself.

The Hidden Man of the Heart

In the New Testament, we are told of this secret place within our existence. The Apostle Peter called it the "hidden man of the heart." In doing so, he employed a Greek word that is quite colorful.

1 Peter 3:4 But let it be the hidden man of the heart, in that which is not corruptible, even the ornament of a meek and quiet spirit, which is in the sight of God of great price.

The Greek word *kruptos* is one that speaks of a secret, or a hidden point of vulnerability. In modern vernacular, most people are aware of the comic book hero named Superman. His only weakness involved an element called kryptonite, a stone brought from the planet of his origin called Krypton. While this is a fanciful tale of science fiction, it utilized the ideal of the Greek word *kruptos.*

There is a secret place within you and me where the echoes of the point of our true origin are distinctly heard. The Word of God tells of the secret place where He dwells: the point from which the still small voice of the Almighty is whispered to the ears of our heart.

The Apostle Paul wrote to the church at Corinth and detailed the target point of this secret place within every person. Regarding the ministry of prophetic insight, Paul said that the church should speak prophetically into the hearts of those entering their place of meeting..

*1 **Corinthians** 14:25 And thus are the secrets of his heart made manifest; and so falling down on his face he will worship God, and report that God is in you of a truth.*

When the hidden man of the heart is touched, he will react in worshipful expression before God. It might be that this is the place being made vibrant when we are "born again" through the blood of Jesus. Prior to our being "born" in the natural, we were hidden in a secret place within our mother. We were alive, but not yet born. Being born again would have to include this idea of coming out from the hidden and manifesting in the breath of life.

If we are born again, we have an obligation to keep on breathing. One big gulp of air at birth does not keep a baby alive for very long in the natural. In similar fashion, the gasp of the breath of life brought to you during a salvation experience must be exchanged on a continuing basis for us to remain vibrant.

There are so many ways that this insight can be applied to our walk in the spirit. Without a steady supply of oxygen, the brain ceases to function. In order to continually move within the power of the mind of Christ, we must enjoy a steady stream of the breath of God within us.

To All Mankind

Knowing every person is created with these factors within them offers to us a fresh understanding of how God relates to man. Often we grapple with the thought of individuals having never heard of the saving power of belief in the Lord Jesus Christ. We might think of those raised in a seemingly impossible social environment, and wonder if such a person has ever really enjoyed an opportunity of experiencing God. Or what of the scenario involving a remote tribe or culture not in the mainstream of modern communication or information exchange?

In the Book of Romans, we discover that the invisible things of God are clearly seen by every individual in the world. In fact, God says that they are "clearly seen," leaving no doubt for misinterpretation.

Romans 1:19-20 Because that which may be known of God is manifest in them; for God hath shewed it unto them. ²⁰ For

7

the invisible things of him from the creation of the world are clearly seen, being understood by the things that are made, even his eternal power and Godhead; so that they are without excuse:

Every person breathing at this moment is lit with the presence of God. Something within each individual can see God, and there is some way the light of God is shining within the innermost places of each life.

When a person breathes, it is an indication of the searching of the light of God within them. It is also a sign of the Almighty showing Himself within the life of the person. No one can rightfully say they have an excuse for not knowing God. I am not saying this is a mode to salvation, as Jesus is the only road to the Heavenly Father. What am I declaring is the truth of the Word of God. When someone seeks for the Lord, He will be found of them. This is plain gospel. Consider what God did for Cornelius and for Silas on the road to Damascus. God knows how to present Himself to someone earnestly dealing with this measure of godliness within their heart.

In the Bible, whenever the nostrils are cited, closeness or a measure of intimate friendship is indicated. Job spoke of the fact that while he breathed, the presence of God continually attempted to draw near in friendship and tender love. Each natural breath paved the way for the visitation of the nearness of the Spirit of God to him.

Job 27:3 All the while my breath (n'shammah) is in me, and the spirit (ruwach) of God is in my nostrils;

For Job, a man enduring horrific challenges in life, the breath of existence was matched by the visitation of the presence of

God. If anyone would have had legitimate argument for whether or not to accept fellowship with God, it might have been Job. The circumstances of His life were horrific at times. In the midst of every difficulty, Job was ever cognizant of the presence of the Most High.

An Invitation to You

There are many things to be said concerning the breath of God, and regarding the ways He desires to move in demonstrations of His Spirit. Within this book, we will explore the varied facets of the breath of God as He partners with His children. Primarily focusing upon the Old Testament, we will explore many aspects of the intent of God for His people.

The church is supposed to be filled with the Spirit, or breath of God. May the Lord establish the true meaning of this within our life and ministries. God created the church to be a source of His breath upon the face of humanity, as well as upon the place where we have been given life. We are filled with His wind, and that wind needs to flow through us.

The last verse in the Psalms spoke of the best usage of the breath of life. Everything breathing must praise the Lord. Not just people, but everything must praise the Lord if there is breath within them.

Psalm 150:6 Let every thing that hath breath (n'shammah) praise the Lord. Praise ye the Lord.

Let us allow the breath of life to illumine an understanding of what God is saying to us in this writing. Knowing the truth sets us free. As we have learned these initial lessons concerning the breath within us, it would be prudent for us to ask God at this very moment to begin to speak deeply with us.

If you have never asked Jesus Christ to be your savior, you can give your life to Him right now. Speak to God, and tell Him that you accept His Son as the Lord of your life. Ask for the forgiveness that can only come through the blood that Jesus shed at the Cross of Calvary. Commit your life to God, and begin to enjoy the life you were created to know in Him.

May the light of the Lord within our being shine brightly, and may His presence make itself known to our very hearts.

Chapter 1

The *Ruwach* of God

In the Old Testament, the Hebrew word *ruwach* is the term best defining the expression of the person of God Almighty. On every occasion this particular word is utilized, the ideal of the heart and individuality of God is conveyed. Whenever the Spirit of the Lord is mentioned in the Old Covenant it is always the *ruwach* of the Lord.

In the beginning of the Book of Genesis, we discern a quite compelling scene. After the rebellion of Satan, the earth was reduced to a state of disarray and darkness. The Bible tells us this *ruwach* of God moved upon the face of the waters of this planet.

Genesis 1:2 And the earth was without form, and void; and darkness was upon the face of the deep. And the Spirit of God moved upon the face of the waters.

The Hebrew word translated as "moved" is a rarely used word speaking of a bird fluttering over its young. Quite literally, the personality of God was moving upon this creation with a sense of brooding and intense watching. There is the idea of the offering of tender care and the contemplation of what should be done to restore.

As noted in the introduction of this book, God created man through the investment of Himself within Adam and Eve. In the "cool" of each day, God would come down into the Garden of

Eden and extend Himself to these two. Our vernacular might interpret the "cool of the day" as being a time in the early morning or evening when the sun in the sky is not as hot. In this passage, the word translated as "cool" is the word *ruwach*. This means God Himself came to commune with them in the very presence of His heart.

> *Genesis 3:8 And they heard the voice of the Lord God walking in the garden in the cool of the day: and Adam and his wife hid themselves from the presence of the Lord God amongst the trees of the garden.*

It is a phenomenal thing to read of Adam and Eve hiding from this wondrous presence. Granted, Adam and Eve had just committed a measure of rebellion and betrayal, and because of this they hid themselves from the person of God. We do not know how many days, or years in human factoring, God fellowshipped with Adam and Eve. They knew Him and had no reason to flee from His personality.

While we might find this rejection of God somewhat perplexing in the distant lens of our modern perception, we must recognize there are millions of people hiding from the presence of God everyday. In Genesis 6, God said He would not always strive with this rejection of His heart. At some point, the invitation of the Spirit of God will end concerning mankind.

> *Genesis 6:3 And the Lord said, My <u>spirit</u> shall not always strive with man, for that he also is flesh: yet his days shall be an hundred and twenty years.*

According to Isaiah 57, God will extend His heart to the humble and contrite. Included in this wonderful equation is a

12

promise for the contrite, as they are to dwell with God in His holy place.

Isaiah 57:15-16 For thus saith the high and lofty One that inhabiteth eternity, whose name is Holy; I dwell in the high and holy place, with him also that is of a contrite and humble spirit, to revive the spirit (ruwach) of the humble, and to revive the heart of the contrite ones. [16] For I will not contend for ever, neither will I be always wroth: for the spirit (ruwach) should fail before me, and the souls (n'shammah) which I have made.

Contrition is a state of humility wherein we become as finely ground dust. The Bible tells us man was made from the dust of the ground. We are not formed from the soil or from the dirt, but from the dust of the ground. This is significant because dust is not something merely "left-over" from a project. This type of contrite dust had to be fashioned in a creative manner. It cost something of God to form the dust, and there was the measure of His heart invested into shaping mankind.

Genesis 2:7 And the Lord God formed man of the dust of the ground, and breathed into his nostrils the breath of life; and man became a living soul.

If we desire to be caught up into the breath of God, we must return to the state of dust-like existence where we can be easily caught by the slightest wind of His presence. Whenever we are contrite, we are able to flow with God Himself. It is not an issue of being influenced by Him, but of depicting Him. There is quite a difference between being a part of Him and being alongside Him. Any ruffian can be knocked off balance by a gust of wind. A building can be shaken by a blast of air. It takes a sensitive heart to be moved by the breeze of His whisper.

A Description of the Ruwach

A rare glimpse of the *ruwach* is provided by the illustrative portrayals of Ezekiel. In the following verse, the *ruwach* of God is described as a whirlwind, a massive cloud enfolding itself in great brightness.

Ezekiel 1:4 And I looked, and, behold, a whirlwind came out of the north, a great cloud, and a fire infolding itself, and a brightness was about it, and out of the midst thereof as the colour of amber, out of the midst of the fire.

The breath of God is phenomenal in scope, and this was the depiction afforded to the eye of Ezekiel. Whether God represents Himself in the billowing whirlwind, or in the form of the still small voice, He remains the Almighty God of all things.

Another rare insight is seen in the depiction of the living creatures of God as they relate to the breath of God. These beings move with the *ruwach* in flawless fashion, as they are comprised of the *ruwach* itself.

Ezekiel 1:20-21 Whithersoever the spirit was to go, they went, thither was their spirit to go; and the wheels were lifted up over against them: for the spirit of the living creature was in the wheels. [21] When those went, these went; and when those stood, these stood; and when those were lifted up from the earth, the wheels were lifted up over against them: for the spirit of the living creature was in the wheels.

Take note of the fact that the living creatures are totally comprised of the spirit of God and they move effortlessly in tandem with Him. The *ruwach* of the creatures was in their ability to turn and move wherever the heart of God desired to go.

Psalm 8:5 proclaimed man is made a little lower, or a bit less, than the angels.

Psalm 8:5 For thou hast made him a little lower than the angels, and hast crowned him with glory and honour.

Since the *ruwach* of God is also within man, could this mean angels are comprised of the *ruwach* of God, while man has a deposit of the *ruwach* within? These angelic beings are comprised of the very character of God. Man has to choose to honor Godly character, but as he makes this choice he will be crowned with glory and honor.

According to the word of the Lord through Ezekiel, the heart of the unredeemed is as a stone. Stone will reflect light in a profound manner, and the image of God can be seen without any hindrance. God promised to give a heart of flesh, capable of interacting with the presence of God.

Ezekiel 36:26-27 A new heart also will I give you, and a new spirit will I put within you: and I will take away the stony heart out of your flesh, and I will give you an heart of flesh. [27] And I will put my spirit within you, and cause you to walk in my statutes, and ye shall keep my judgments, and do them.

This new heart is certainly a description of what Jesus said concerning the process of life in God. The breath of God must be acted upon within us in order for us to know God and the things of His Spirit.

John 3:5-6 Jesus answered, Verily, verily, I say unto thee, Except a man be born of water and of the Spirit, he cannot enter into the kingdom of God. [6] That which is born of the flesh is flesh; and that which is born of the Spirit is spirit.

15

Being born again with a new heart is grand, but even the new heart within us will not profit anything if it is not continually functioning within the auspices of the Spirit of God.

John 6:63 It is the spirit that quickeneth; the flesh profiteth nothing: the words that I speak unto you, they are spirit, and they are life.

A View of the Temple in Heaven

When we read of the men and women of Biblical fame, it is easy to imagine that they were granted some special measure of access to the things of God. How often we forget that Elijah did not know the blood of Jesus, and neither did Daniel or Joseph or Ezekiel.

We as children of God should thrive in the places defined in the Bible. Our experiences in God should rival, or exceed, what is listed within the pages of the Old Testament. Jesus told His followers that the same works that he did would be done by us. Even greater works than His will be done, and that is quite a humbling prospect.

Ezekiel was an incredible prophet of God. Throughout his writings, we find that the *ruwach* of God would lift him into the heavens, and would also take Him from place to place upon the earth. Elijah also enjoyed this supernatural transportation system, as did Philip in the Book of Acts.

Upon one journey into the heavens, Ezekiel experienced something of dynamic import. As he was with an angel, the measuring of the Temple in Heaven was being conducted. In the narrative, the walls of the Temple were said to be constructed of the *ruwach* of God.

Ezekiel 42:16-20 He measured the east side with the measuring reed, five hundred reeds, with the measuring reed round about. [17] He measured the north side, five hundred reeds, with the measuring reed round about. [18] He measured the south side, five hundred reeds, with the measuring reed. [19] He turned about to the west side, and measured five hundred reeds with the measuring reed. [20] He measured it by the four sides: it had a wall round about, five hundred reeds long, and five hundred broad, to make a separation between the sanctuary and the profane place.

Why is this insight significant for us? Everything that we do upon the earth should be focused upon what happens at the Throne of God in Heaven, and in conjunction with the Temple of the Tabernacle of Testimony. The walls of this place are comprised of the breath of God, indicating that everything transpiring within is based upon the movement of His breath.

As we are dust in the wind of God, the Spirit can take us anywhere that He so desires. The Bible said that the Spirit of God blows wherever He wants, and no man can dictate the course. If we in the natural attempt to put the wind in a box, it ceases to be wind and becomes mere air. The wind of God moves our heart back and forth, in and out, up and down according to the mind of His Spirit.

The Ruwach Upon

Whenever the Bible speaks of the Spirit of the Lord coming upon or being put upon someone, the *ruwach* is always employed. What does this mean, seeing every man is already invested with the *ruwach* of God? The obvious answer is found in Isaiah 61.

17

Isaiah 61:1-3 The Spirit of the Lord God is upon me; because the Lord hath anointed me to preach good tidings unto the meek; he hath sent me to bind up the brokenhearted, to proclaim liberty to the captives, and the opening of the prison to them that are bound; ² To proclaim the acceptable year of the Lord, and the day of vengeance of our God; to comfort all that mourn; ³ To appoint unto them that mourn in Zion, to give unto them beauty for ashes, the oil of joy for mourning, the garment of praise for the spirit of heaviness; that they might be called trees of righteousness, the planting of the Lord, that he might be glorified.

Jesus cited this passage when he proclaimed the beginning of His earthly ministry. Obviously, the Savior was functioning according to the deposit of *ruwach* within Him. He was fully God, but also fully man. When the point of ministry was required of Him, the Lord received a coming upon of the *ruwach* of God empowering Him to do the work of His Father in Heaven.

Whenever the *ruwach* of God "comes upon" someone, an anointing is activated or imparted to represent the very person of God. Consider the case of Gideon as an example.

Judges 6:34 But the Spirit of the Lord came upon Gideon, and he blew a trumpet; and Abi-ezer was gathered after him.

In the case of the cited passage from Judges, the *ruwach* came upon Gideon as a cloak. The intent accompanying the visitation of the *ruwach* will vary from instance to instance in the Word. The *ruwach* of the Lord will manifest itself in differing ways. The following are some Scriptural examples of what might occur when the *ruwach* of the Lord visits someone:

18

Broods	Genesis 1:2
Fills, furnishes	Exodus 31:3
Exists, Comes to pass	Numbers 24:2
Carries away	Ezekiel 11:24
To agitate, bore	Judges 13:25
Push forward	Judges 14:6
Speaks	II Samuel 23:2
Pick up, re-locate	I Kings 18:12
Dwell with, upon	Isaiah 11:2
Blow upon, disperse	Isaiah 40:7
Move elsewhere	Ezekiel 37:1
Filled with Judgment and Power	Micah 3:8

The *ruwach* of God will do whatever is necessary to invigorate and direct the individual in partnership with the purpose of God. There are times in the Word when the *ruwach* will manifest in ways totally independent of the hand of man. God will show Himself in the characteristic power that once brooded upon the face of the deep in the accounts of Genesis.

Winds of War

In the case of the destruction of the Egyptian army within the miracle of the Red Sea, the phenomenon was attributed to the work of the *ruwach* of God. Imagine God Himself acting in visible fashion against the hosts of Egypt.

In the issue of the plague of locusts, the Bible indicates the breath of God brought a massive swarm of locusts into the nation of Egypt. Imagine the character of God coordinating and sending these locusts against the greatest nation in the known world.

Exodus 10:13 And Moses stretched forth his rod over the land of Egypt, and the Lord brought an east wind upon the land all that day, and all that night; and when it was morning, the east wind brought the locusts.

As Pharaoh and his army pursued Moses and the children of Israel into the Red Sea, Pharaoh was oblivious to the fact that the ruwach of God was the operative force suspending the parted waters. Neither did he consider the nostrils of God as communicating the tenderness and nearness of His care to the fleeing people.

Exodus 15:8 And with the blast of thy nostrils the waters were gathered together, the floods stood upright as an heap, and the depths were congealed in the heart of the sea.

Since God was on the scene, He directed the Israelites safely through the seabed, and then His breath released the waters back to their original depth. Effectively, the army of Pharaoh was destroyed by the most personal dimension of the breath of God.

Exodus 15:10 Thou didst blow with thy wind, the sea covered them: they sank as lead in the mighty waters.

God also released a destroying *ruwach* against Babylon. This corrupting influence was not only devastating in power, but also corrosive in its effect.

Jeremiah 51:1 Thus saith the Lord; Behold, I will raise up against Babylon, and against them that dwell in the midst of them that rise up against me, a destroying wind;

The *ruwach* of God will chase and drive away the enemies standing against the people of God. Like a whirlwind, the presence of God will sweep clean the vestiges of enemy encampment.

Isaiah 17:13 The nations shall rush like the rushing of many waters: but God shall rebuke them, and they shall flee far off, and shall be chased as the chaff of the mountains before the wind, and like a rolling thing before the whirlwind.

In the Book of Psalms, an intriguing passage connects the breath of God with the angels of the Lord. Imagine the combined efforts of the breath of God and an angelic pursuer as they drive away a resisting enemy.

Psalm 35:5 Let them be as chaff before the wind: and let the angel of the Lord chase them.

God stands strong on behalf of those laboring together with Him for the cause of righteousness. It is difficult to perceive how the presence of God can move in such devastating ways. We have not readily seen these types of visitations, but they are readily spoken of in the Word. God never changes, and He has promised to powerfully defend His children.

In fact, God can stir up the *ruwach* within individuals in positions of authority of foreign lands. In times when God desires to impact the nations, he can certainly cause His nature to become evident within individuals, as is the case with the Kings of the Medes and of King Cyrus.

Jeremiah 51:11 Make bright the arrows; gather the shields: the Lord hath raised up the spirit (ruwach) of the kings of the Medes: for his device is against Babylon, to destroy it; because it is the vengeance of the Lord, the vengeance of his temple.

Ezra 1:1 Now in the first year of Cyrus king of Persia, that the word of the Lord by the mouth of Jeremiah might be fulfilled, the Lord stirred up the spirit (ruwach) of Cyrus king of Persia, that he made a proclamation throughout all his kingdom, and put it also in writing, saying,

There will be times in our ministry that God will stir up the spirit of Presidents and leaders of countries. Sometimes the favor of the Lord will be impressed upon the leader, as was the anointing that came upon Cyrus. God will do whatever is necessary to empower the mission delivered to His sons.

Sons

In Old Testament times, the ruwach of God was continually "poured out" upon the people. The individuals upon whom the Spirit of God would pour would either accept or reject Him. Sadly, the latter was most often the human response to the benevolence of love from God.

Ezekiel 39:29 Neither will I hide my face any more from them: for I have poured out my spirit upon the house of Israel, saith the Lord God.

In this passage, God told Ezekiel that He would visit mankind in such a way as to allow for knowledge of Him and His ways. All flesh would have the privilege of knowing Him through the redemptive work of Jesus. The promise of the Father for us today is listed in Joel 2 and Acts 2. God promised to pour out His person, or *ruwach*, upon all flesh and upon servants and handmaids. Can you imagine this assurance as being one of God pouring out Himself upon people? What a glorious pledge of love.

> *Joel 2:28-29 And it shall come to pass afterward, that I will pour out my spirit upon all flesh; and your sons and your daughters shall prophesy, your old men shall dream dreams, your young men shall see visions: [29] And also upon the servants and upon the handmaids in those days will I pour out my spirit.*

The *ruwach* of God is literally poured out to the degree that His presence drenches the recipient. This visitation empowers our dream and visions, our prophetic insights and the commissioning of our ministry unto the Heavenly Father.

Another famous passage is found within the pages of the Book of Zechariah. In this magnificent statement, we are assured it is not power or authority, but relationship with God Himself that brings the victory of our faith.

> *Zechariah 4:6 Then he answered and spake unto me, saying, This is the word of the Lord unto Zerubbabel, saying, Not by might, nor by power, but by my spirit, saith the Lord of hosts.*

Elijah had accomplished many fabulous things in partnership with God. At a transitional point for the man of God, the Almighty met with the prophet on Mt. Horeb. Herein we discover a key to partnering with God.

> *1 Kings 19:11-12 And he said, Go forth, and stand upon the mount before the Lord. And, behold, the Lord passed by, and a great and strong wind rent the mountains, and brake in pieces the rocks before the Lord; but the Lord was not in the wind:*

and after the wind an earthquake; but the Lord was not in the earthquake: [12] *And after the earthquake a fire; but the Lord was not in the fire: and after the fire a still small voice.*

God appeared before Elijah with shaking, with fire and with His *ruwach* in an attempt to persuade Him to keep moving forward in tandem with purpose. The Word says God was not in the fire, the earthquake or even in the *ruwach*. What does this mean? How could God not "be" in His person? The answer is simple. God does not come solely to fellowship with His people or to demonstrate the power of His presence. These glorious things are not enough to satisfy the intent of God for mankind if they are bereft of the commitment of man to His purpose.

We know this principle in our own existence. Have you ever been someplace, but not really be there? Have you ever been a part of something unfulfilling and the investment of yourself was lacking. God is never disinterested, but the visitation of His presence does not necessarily guarantee His Heart is activated in a matter. Before you become too exasperated over this statement, remember God is omnipresent.

At this very moment, God is aware of some incredibly vile scenarios. Yet, the heart of God might not be activated and in operation within those situations. If this can be true when it comes to evil, can it also be true when it comes to the atmosphere surrounding a disinterested person. Elijah was anything but concerned about what God wanted to accomplish at this moment on Mt. Horeb.

Elijah was instructed by the still small voice to wrap himself in his mantle, representing his calling, and to stand afresh before God. Relationship, even with the Almighty, without the commitment to His will and ways is not sufficient. God wants His people to be lovers and warriors, friends and fellow-laborers.

In our ongoing discussions about the breath of God, we must always remember God is interested in the development of you as a child and a son. This is His continual passion, and He is adamant about fulfilling this ultimate agenda. You are a treasure to Him, and He strongly desires that you find the fullness of His heart within yours.

Our prayer should echo the heartfelt sentiment of King David when he implored God to remain with him in intimate expression of *ruwach.*

Psalm 51:10 Create in me a clean heart, O God; and renew a right spirit within me.

May the presence of our God cause our heart to be continually sensitive to the fresh expression of His breath!

Chapter 2

Nuwach

The believer will often associate the concept of rest with refreshment from weariness. While this meaning has merit within the context of human existence, it has no bearing when considering the capacities of God. The Word of God plainly says God does not sleep and is not wearied.

> *Isaiah 40:28 Hast thou not known? hast thou not heard, that the everlasting God, the Lord, the Creator of the ends of the earth, fainteth not, neither is weary? there is no searching of his understanding.*

> *Psalm 121:2-4 My help cometh from the Lord, which made heaven and earth. ³ He will not suffer thy foot to be moved: he that keepeth thee will not slumber. ⁴ Behold, he that keepeth Israel shall neither slumber nor sleep.*

People regularly view God from the perspective of their own frailty. When God speaks of a Sabbath rest, we might be inclined to envision His Throne as an easy chair. We might concoct thoughts of the Ancient of Days as if He is a Father Time figure, preparing to collapse from exhaustion at any moment.

These are ridiculous assessments, and might not even remotely depict your thoughts concerning the "rest" of God. In reality, we must all adjust our thinking concerning the proper assessment of how God intends for us to enter into His rest.

27

Creation

> *Genesis 2:2-3 And on the seventh day God ended his work which he had made; and he rested (shabath) on the seventh day from all his work which he had made. [3] And God blessed the seventh day, and sanctified it: because that in it he had rested (shabath) from all his work which God created and made.*

The first mention of the word "rest" in the Bible defined the moment when God ceased the progression of creation on the seventh day. The Hebrew word translated as "rest" is the expression from which the word Sabbath is derived. We are told God blessed and made holy this day. The Sabbath is a day of active blessing, a time when the holy purpose of God is contemplated and activated. As the first "rest" involved God, and God alone, it could not have been for the cause of exhaustion and need of replenishment.

The progression of seven in the Bible is always one detailing the measure of the ways of God. The idea of the seventh day is one of blessing and preparatory equipping. It is one speaking of the completion of a task, a reflection of the euphoria associated with the successful venture, and a joyful anticipation of the beginning of a new and fresh work.

Romans 9:28-29 declares that God will "finish the work, and cut it short in righteousness: because a short work will the Lord make upon the earth," the Lord speaks of a contract that will be honored quickly. The passage continues by stating "the Lord of Sabaoth had left us a seed," referring to the *sperma* of God, or original and personalized intent of God for this creation. Combining the topics of rest, Sabbath and Sabaoth, we must come to the realization that the issue in the heart of God is one of restoring the purpose of His creation.

The Sabbath was never intended to be a day of inactivity, but one of reflection, supply and proactive preparation. The Sabbath was not designed for restrictive rules and prohibitions, but rather the promise of empowerment and progressive thought.

God was forced to introduce the regulations of the Sabbath because the people had failed in their pursuit of His intention for the seventh day. The Pharisees, instead of empowering the people toward a positive application of the purpose-driven desire of the Lord for the Sabbath, imposed increasing restrictions upon the people in an attempt to be pleasing to God on this seventh day.

When I was a boy, I gained a taste of the gentile equivalent of the Pharisaic constraints regarding the Sabbath. Measures of "holiness" were applied to rules and morals of acceptable behavior for Sundays. Although Sunday was not really the seventh day, we still remained largely inactive on Sundays in an effort to somehow be pleasing to God. I was not even permitted to throw a ball on Sunday when I was a child, all because God wanted us to do nothing but go to church on the Sabbath.

When I became a Pastor and recognized I did more work on Sunday than on any other day of the week, I wondered about the seeming contradiction of the supposed "day of rest." What about the Mom or Grandma rushing home at the request of their husband on Sunday to fry chicken on the day of rest. This was done so everyone could come home from church, overeat and take a nap in order for God to be pleased?

During football season in America, churches demand their Pastors release the worshippers from morning service in plenty of time for the congregation to get home, eat and watch the NFL on television for the further glory of God. In Dallas, believers even claim that the football stadium has a hole in the roof so that God can watch the Cowboys on the Sabbath. Somehow, something is askew.

The Sabbath is a day for seeking God, and for gaining His heartbeat for spiritual direction. The ultimate goal is in partnering with Him as a son for His intentions upon the earth. It might be better for us to consider the Sabbath to be our busiest day, as we are to be caught up into the presence of the Lord God for the purpose of being instructed and energized for the purpose of the Kingdom.

In the twentieth chapter of Exodus, there is an additional reference to the seventh day. God utilized a distinct Hebrew expression, *nuwach*, to define the idea of the Sabbath rest. Within this divine perspective, we again perceive the Sabbath was blessed and set apart for the Holy purpose of God.

Exodus 20:11 *For in six days the Lord made heaven and earth, the sea, and all that in them is, and rested the seventh day: wherefore the Lord blessed the sabbath day, and hallowed it.*

The ultimate measure of sonship is found whenever the breath of God is actively resting upon a person. When God rests in lively fashion, it is indicative of the Hebrew word *nuwach*. This is the measure of partnering with God according to what He has done, and what He is continuing to do. How do we engage God in this fashion? The prospect of this existence is much more accessible than we might imagine.

Firstfruits

In the Book of Ezekiel, we observe a defining principle of *nuwach*, or the actively abiding breath of God. This measure of definition has to do with a concept well known to Pentecostals. The Lord declared the *nuwach* would be offered to those existing in the pathway of firstfruits.

Ezekiel 44:30 And the first of all the firstfruits of all things, and every oblation of all, of every sort of your oblations, shall be the priest's: ye shall also give unto the priest the first of your dough, that he may cause the blessing to rest in thine house.

The firstfruits offering should be one familiar to Pentecostals, for the church was birthed on the Day of Pentecost. Pentecost is also known by the term "firstfruits." Firstfruits is not a tithe or an offering, even though it is regularly confused with these expressions of giving. A firstfruits is a giving of the best of the best, and is independent of any other donation to the work of the Lord. It touches the heart of your passion so you can appeal to the heart of the passion of God.

Pentecostals are called to be firstfruits before the Heavenly Father. The church should offer to God those things extraordinary, and not merely those required (tithe) or discretionary (offering). The gift of the Father was given on the Feast of Firstfruits, and it speaks of what God continues to offer in Sabbath existence. Sadly, many are called but few choose the calling. Millions call themselves Pentecostals, but only a percentage of these people seek the deeper things of partnering with God. Their pursuit of God is not focused upon the new, but upon the old. This is not Sabbath intent, and it does not truly please the heart of the Heavenly Father.

Isaiah 28:11-12 For with stammering lips and another tongue will he speak to this people. [12] To whom he said, This is the rest wherewith ye may cause the weary to rest; and this is the refreshing: yet they would not hear.

The Word of God tells us whenever a person speaks in an unknown tongue, in the spirit they are speaking mysteries (I Corinthians 14:2). Mysteries, or *musterion* in the Greek, are heretofore unknown dimensions of the plan of God. Those speaking in "stammering lips and unknown tongues" must know this is firstfruits language. It cannot be separated from the ongoing dimension of partnering with God for the new.

Not only does God abide within these children, but he also promised a "refreshing." This is the Hebrew word *raga,* and it has a meaning of doing something quickly or decisively. The word is utilized to describe a wink, or a quick toss of some sort. Therefore, God offered the opportunity for His sons to accomplish things quickly. The action also implies a briskness that is associated with confidence and an overall good mood.

Look again at Ezekiel 44, and notice the person engaged in firstfruits relationship with God will know the active breath of the Lord upon his household. The power of His active and attending breath will engender fear within the encampment of the enemy forces positioned near to us.

Deuteronomy 25:19 Therefore it shall be, when the Lord thy God hath given thee <u>rest</u> from all thine enemies round about, in the land which the Lord thy God giveth thee for an inheritance to possess it, that thou shalt blot out the *remembrance of Amalek from under heaven; thou shalt not forget it.*

The *nuwach* of God is so fearsome to the enemy and to his forces because they recognize they will soon be driven from the places of divine inheritance. The firstfruits people give their best to God, and He dwells within them. The foul nature of the enemy cannot defeat the breath of God standing in active measure upon the households of the saints.

The Leader in Warfare

Amalek was mentioned in the previously cited passage of Scripture. God particularly had distaste for this group of people, for they deceitfully withstood the advance of the people of God into the land of promise. A classic battle is detailed in the Word of God wherein Moses stood at the top of a hill while the armies of Israel battled against Amalek in the valley below.

Exodus 17:11 And it came to pass, when Moses held up his hand, that Israel prevailed: and when he let down his hand, Amalek prevailed.

Look at this sequence of events once again, and interpret it now in light of what we have just learned about *nuwach*. Moses became wearied in the natural and stepped out of the depiction of the abiding breath, or *nuwach* of the Lord. The attendant breath of God was communicated upon Moses as He stood upon the promise of purpose, and this is also our mandate of responsibility in the continuing battle for righteousness..

We must surround ourselves with righteous armor on the right and left, just as Moses did. Victory cannot possibly be achieved if we allow ourselves to attempt the work in our own strength. It will not be accomplished if we allow ourselves to be unequally yoked with those not believing in the same purpose of God. Two can put ten thousand to flight, and we must remember God chooses to move this way at myriad times.

God will lead His people into the places of their dominion. It is vital for the people to recognize the directive of the Lord for their life and ministry. This principle of standing in the midst of the planting of the Lord is imperative for victory. The promise in the Book of Isaiah is whenever we stand on behalf of His purpose, the *nuwach* of the Lord will be made available upon us.

> *Isaiah 30:32 And in every place where the grounded staff shall pass, which the Lord shall lay upon him, it shall be with tabrets and harps: and in battles of shaking will he fight with it.*

Wherever the *nuwach* is present, the potential of overwhelming triumph exists. The sons of God must recognize the principles of partnering with God. If we will be faithful in this way, God will not fail us. Watchfulness is the order of the day, as the *nuwach* of the Lord will require we remain in absolute devotion to the ways of God. The *nuwach* was upon the children of Israel until such time as they complained about the purpose of God. Reflect upon the scenario detailed for us in the following verses.

> *Numbers 10:34-11:3 And the cloud of the Lord was upon them by day, when they went out of the camp. [35] And it came to pass, when the ark set forward, that Moses said, Rise up, Lord, and let thine enemies be scattered; and let them that hate thee flee before thee. [36] And when it rested, he said, Return, O Lord, unto the many thousands of Israel. 11:1 And when the people complained, it displeased the Lord: and the Lord heard*

it; and his anger was kindled; and the fire of the Lord burnt among them, and consumed them that were in the uttermost parts of the camp. [2] And the people cried unto Moses; and when Moses prayed unto the Lord, the fire was quenched. [3] And he called the name of the place Taberah: because the fire of the Lord burnt among them.

In the presence of all the people, Moses verbally detailed the principle we have just been contemplating. The abiding presence of the breath of God had been disregarded by the people, and they complained about the ways of the Most High. A unique thing happened as the fire of the Lord moved quickly throughout the camp of murmurers.

There is something marvelous within the telling of this event and it bears explanation. The Lord Sabaoth is also known in the Bible as the Lord of Hosts, the representation of the armies of God moving within the framework of the Spirit of Judgment and Burning. When the fire of God progressed through the camp, it was a sign of how God and His angelic host displayed themselves on behalf of the *nuwach*. As the *nuwach* comes upon the vanguard people of the heart of God, each person must guard against the infiltration of personal ingratitude, as it can often be the tangible expression of evil intent from the enemy.

Lord Sabaoth will partner with the sons of God. These privileged ones are offered the promise of the power of companionship with the breath of God. There must never be a moment when this is disputed within the camp of the saints. Such action is highly improper, and extremely dangerous.

A magnificent example of the *ruwach* nature of God when He settled in *nuwach* fashion is seen in the ministry of Ezekiel. The *ruwach* of God carried this man of God into a valley of dry bones. Ezekiel then enjoyed the nuwach of God as it settled upon him, and he entered in to an active point of standing in the place of miracle power.

> *Ezekiel 37:1 The hand of the Lord was upon me, and carried me out in the spirit (ruwach) of the Lord, and set me down in the midst of the valley which was full of bones,*

God will regularly place us into situations where we are surrounded by enemy forces or impossible situations. If we are called of the Lord to be there, He will be present with us in the midst of the challenge. We often forget that the table of the Lord is spread in the presence of our enemies.

The Lord promised to be with us in the valley of the shadow of death, although we do not look forward to the prospect. Sometimes it would appear death is all around us in the valley. If God has carried us or led us into such a circumstance, He will be with us there. Observe the manner of God partnering with Ezekiel.

> *Ezekiel 37:9-10 Then said he unto me, Prophesy unto the wind (ruwach), prophesy, son of man, and say to the wind (ruwach), Thus saith the Lord God; Come from the four winds (ruwach), O breath (ruwach), and breathe (naphak) upon these slain, that they may live. [10] So I prophesied as he commanded me, and the breath (ruwach) came into them, and they lived, and stood up upon their feet, an exceeding great army.*

Could Ezekiel have been prophesying to the *ruwach* of the presence of God Himself, or was he prophesying to the power of a *ruwach* expression? Whichever the case, the man of God was able to represent the very presence of the Lord in the midst of a miracle.

It would seem for every opportunity of *nuwach*, there is an opposing opportunity for fear or criticism. Any human could muster words of complaint if they found themselves positioned in a valley of dry bones. There would be no shortage of words to describe the hopeless nature of such a prospect. The mind of humanity could fashion entire paragraphs of complaint to express the disfavor of being in such a climate.

We might even be able to form some reasonable arguments before God, just in case He was unaware of the actual position into where we were placed. It takes a person of devoted purpose to speak what God wants to do in such a situation, in spite of assessments from the perspective of humanity.

Both of these options can occur in our appointment before the Lord. This fact is an awesome privilege and responsibility for the child of God. The ultimate point of answer was when a powerful burst of wind came upon this gathering of bones, and the *ruwach* of God entered into this army. Magnificent!

Impartation of Mantle and Anointing

It is apparent God will at times direct individuals to impart the *nuwach* into others functioning within the same camp of purpose. This was the case with Moses as the *nuwach* was imparted to the seventy elders and unto Eldad and Medad.

Numbers 11:25-26 And the Lord came down in a cloud, and spake unto him, and took of the spirit (ruwach) that was upon him, and gave it unto the seventy elders: and it came to pass, that, when the spirit rested (nuwach) upon them, they prophesied, and did not cease. [26] But there remained two of the men in the camp, the name of the one was Eldad, and the name of the other Medad: and the spirit (ruwach) rested upon them;

and they were of them that were written, but went not out unto the tabernacle: and they prophesied in the camp.

The same type of impartation occurred within the transfer of the Spirit of God between Elijah and Elisha. Many people focus upon the mantle falling upon Elisha, but it was the *nuwach* of God making the difference. It might easily be said that without the abiding presence of *nuwach*, the mantle or rod will only be a symbolic vestige of former victory or previous anointing.

2 Kings 2:15 And when the sons of the prophets which were to view at Jericho saw him, they said, The spirit (ruwach) of Elijah doth rest (nuwach) on Elisha. And they came to meet him, and bowed themselves to the ground before him

Dispensations of the capacities of the Most High can be imprinted upon an individual, as was spoken of in Isaiah 11. These traits of the mind and heart of God can be personally impressed upon and within individuals. As the *nuwach* of the Lord is established, traits of the Lord God can be seen in the people of His choosing.

Isaiah 11:2 And the spirit (ruwach) of the Lord shall rest (nuwach) upon him, the spirit (ruwach) of wisdom and understanding, the spirit (ruwach) of counsel and might, the spirit (ruwach) of knowledge and of the fear of the Lord;

Mr. Nuwach and the Nacham

When the Ark of Noah settled upon Ararat, it literally was established in *nuwach*. From this lofty location of new beginnings, God gave the opportunity for mankind to pursue the original plan of God for the world.

Genesis 8:4 And the ark rested in the seventh month, on the seventeenth day of the month, upon the mountains of Ararat.

Captain Noah was a unique individual, as his name literally embodied the Hebrew word *nuwach.* This man was the personification of the person who obeyed God, followed Him and committed to the plan of God in fullness. No matter how foolish it seemed, Noah or *nuwach* was there to abide by the commandments of the Lord.

It would seem restoration was the operative word for Noah. Things had gotten out of hand upon the earth, both in a physical sense and in a spiritual one. God determined it was time to start over, or to return to what was originally intended. Take special notice of what God said when *Noah* was born.

Genesis 5:29 And he called his name Noah, saying, This same shall comfort us concerning our work and toil of our hands, because of the ground which the Lord hath cursed.

This is an incredible statement by the Lord God. This man, *nuwach,* would breathe or sigh (*nacham*) unto God. Why? Because of the work and toil of the hands of God upon the ground having been cursed. Think about this statement. Noah was to minister unto God, to breathe after Him in comfort, because of the investment God made in the ground. Not the dust, but the ground.

How many people were saved when the storm hit and the fountains of the deep were broken open? What caused such a small number of people to be preserved? Did Noah spend time evangelizing the fallen ones who were mimicking and mocking him during the years of the construction of the Ark? The animals filled the boat, but only the family of Noah was spared. God Himself shut the door on the Ark.

At the birth of Noah, God called him to breathe after the needs of the Most High. God also said Noah found grace in the eyes of the Lord. In our simplistic thinking, we have thought this means Noah simply "caught a break" from God. Perhaps God just chose Him, and so the "amazing grace" of the Lord was upon him and his family. It was one of those "there but for the grace of God go I" kind of thing, right?

Wrong.

The eyes of the Lord are His ways, and they search for someone to partner with those ways. The eyes of the Lord seek throughout the earth in pursuit of one willing to submit their heart to God in perfect devotion to His purpose.

Grace will always lift something or someone from one place to another. Perhaps it provides a deliverance of some sort, or a promotion. Grace is decided upon when we agree with the assessment of the judgment of God. If we do not embrace His judgment, we cannot flow with His grace. In essence, the same water destroying the people of the earth was the agent of grace raising the Ark of Noah above destruction.

In the days of Noah, mankind was cavorting with principalities and powers of darkness, and committing abominable acts in the sight of God. Their judgment was to do whatever they wanted to do, and to portray repugnance upon the creation of God.

Noah agreed with the heart of God as it lamented concerning this horrid condition. From His birth, Noah breathed, or sighed, on behalf of the Heavenly Father. This point of mourning was not only in the heart of Noah, but in the heart of God. The same

Hebrew word *nacham* displaying the actions of Noah was also employed to describe the movement of the Spirit of God Himself.

Genesis 6:6-8 And it repented (nacham) the Lord that he had made man on the earth, and it grieved him at his heart. ⁷ And the Lord said, I will destroy man whom I have created from the face of the earth; both man, and beast, and the creeping thing, and the fowls of the air; for it repenteth me (nacham) that I have made them. ⁸ But Noah found grace in the eyes of the Lord.

Immediately prior to this statement about grace, God repeated the phrase "it repenteth me" concerning the creation of mankind. The double usage of the Hebrew word *nacham* indicates God created Noah to grieve over the condition of the earth in the same way His Spirit was grieving. Is this not an amazing assessment by God?

The word *nacham* speaks of breathing or sighing in harmony with the desire for things to be restored. Creative function is the desired goal. The word is used on many occasions in the Bible to speak of God "repenting" over an appointment or situation. The confusion concerning this concept is eliminated when we rightfully view the word through the eye of purpose. God is not grieving because He made a mistake, for God does all things well. His Spirit laments the occasion wherein purpose was abandoned, and investment from His heart was mislaid or wrongfully twisted.

Do you recognize the Spirit of the Lord is grieving over His creation in our day? Do you see mankind mimicking the very same things done in the days of Noah? People are going about their lives as if there is no other God but them. In our day, demonic worship is commonplace. It is not just in the dark alleys of our cities, or in some remote grotto of the desert. Turn on your television, and see how many programs depict to our culture the idea of partnering with the demonic. Our culture is saturated with evil.

Jesus prophesied it would be this way. He likened our day to the time of Noah. Do you recall what our Lord and Savior said about the hour in which we live?

> *Matthew 24:37 But as the days of Noe were, so shall also the coming of the Son of man be.*

In light of this prophecy by our Lord Jesus, we must recognize God is calling us to accept covenant responsibility for His purpose upon and within creation. As covenant bearers of the breath of God, we might be commanded to do things that are unseemly in the eyes of the world. This is fine, as God said in His Word that we would be known as a peculiar people. When David danced the Ark of the Covenant into Jerusalem, he was ridiculed for his appearance in doing so. His response was that he was prepared to even be "more vile" in the eyes of the world if it meant the welcoming of the presence of God.

Ezekiel gave to us a prescription of how this should work. We should not question what God requires of us, for this is a reason concerning the actions required by His Spirit.

> *Ezekiel 14:22-23 Yet, behold, therein shall be left a remnant that shall be brought forth, both sons and daughters: behold, they shall come forth unto you, and ye shall see their way and their doings: and ye shall be comforted concerning the evil that I have brought upon Jerusalem, even concerning*

all that I have brought upon it. [23] *And they shall comfort you, when ye see their ways and their doings: and ye shall know that I have not done without cause all that I have done in it, saith the Lord God.*

Did you notice the key words included in this passage? God said a remnant of sons and daughters would be sent forth to demonstrate the ways and acts of God. These mighty ones will *nacham* before the people and the city. They will stand in opposition to the *ra*, or twisted purpose, which existed within Jerusalem.

God intends to use His sons, or the people of purpose embodying His breath, to do this work. David was the pre-eminent example of this principle. In a renowned passage of Scripture, the twenty-third Psalm, devotion to *nacham* is powerfully presented.

Psalm 23:4 Yea, though I walk through the valley of the shadow of death, I will fear no evil: for thou art with me; thy rod and thy staff they comfort me.

David had been sent into the valley of the shadow of death. God sends covenant representatives into such places because the valley should be a plain of fruitfulness, not of fatality. The Lord is with us in these selected moments of faith.

The rod and the staff are said to be instruments of *nacham*, or partnering with the breath of God for His purpose to be reinstated. The rod is a device of power and precise direction. The staff represents appropriate leadership and solution to administrative challenge. Therefore, the power, direction and leadership of the Lord will direct our partnering with Him and His breath. This is a marvelous aspect of aligning with the breath of the Lord in the midst of challenging scenarios requiring change.

These are the days of *nuwach*. Ours is the hour of breathing with God on behalf of the burden of His eyes. Grace is being poured out upon us. It is the day when the Sun of righteousness is arising upon this earth.

You were chosen from the day you were born to breathe with God concerning the burden of His heart. Even the timeframe of God was specific in causing you to have life within this hour. There are things that God has planned to do through you that you alone can accomplish. We must never underestimate the breath of God within us. You were not an accident, and you are not a misplaced individual. It appeared that God found Noah, but the truth is that God knew where Noah was all along. From his birth, God intended for Noah to share the burden of divine intent.

Through Noah and his family came the new beginnings of life upon the earth. The Ark *rested* according to the obedient calling of the man named *rest*. From this place sprang forth the issue of life. From the *nuwach* comes the place of *m'nuwchah*.

Chapter 3

M'nuwchah

God is very much intent upon moving with mankind to accomplish His plans according to the ultimate purpose established at the foundation of the World. The end of days is upon our world, and God is searching for those with perfect hearts, submitted to Him and His ways. As it was with Noah, so it can be with you today.

The intention of God concerning His people is for them to continue to grow and develop in kingdom authority, representing Him and His ways. During our study of this theme, we have learned the breath of God in some very powerful dimensions. The breath, wind or spirit of God:

-gives life to us

-imparts His presence into our frame

-moves us to know and represent Him in authority

-resides upon us in the power of His abiding presence

-partners with us to accomplish the will of His heart

Now we must discover the next dimension of His plan for our life and existence. It is imperative we begin to represent Him as a seasoned and well-trained champion of His Heart. This aspect of our walk is found in a derivative of the Hebrew *nuah*, the root word of *nuwach*.

45

The Hebrew word *m'nuwchah* is one of feminine gender, meaning it is receptive and creative in intent and demonstration. In other words, this word depicts a place wherein a concept or a principle is being expounded upon and creatively manifested.

This concept can be seen by distinguishing the difference between being a warrior anointed by God for an appointed time, as opposed to the warrior or athlete continually depicting the magnificence of the presence of God. *M'nuwchah* is a place wherein quiet confidence and stillness before God is a way of life, and not an anomaly of random occurrence. Like a seasoned athlete that is perfectly content to accelerate in power, or rest in perfect strength. We are called to establish the latter.

God wants a continuing and attendant resting place. He leads us in His rest through the land of promise, with an eye toward the establishment of an attending place of continual rest. Will Rogers, a great American thespian, once said that America was the only country in the world that waited until it was in a war to actual prepare for war. This would seem to be the way it is with most Christians concerning the things of God.

We must not be merely reactive, but proactive to the voice of our God. We should not continually ask God to "come," for He should already be attendant with us in power. This is the presence of God in the *m'nuwchah*.

Moses and Conquest

Although God was leading Israel in miraculous fashion through the wilderness toward the land of promise, the place of continued encampment was not yet found. In the following grouping of Scripture, God gave His *nuwach* throughout the journey leading to the continuing establishment of *m'nuwchah*.

Deuteronomy 12:9-11 For ye are not as yet come to the rest (m'nuwchah) and to the inheritance, which the Lord your God giveth you. [10] But when ye go over Jordan, and dwell in the land which the Lord your God giveth you to inherit, and when he giveth you rest (nuwach) from all your enemies round about, so that ye dwell in safety; [11] Then there shall be a place which the Lord your God shall choose to cause his name to dwell there; thither shall ye bring all that I command you; your burnt offerings, and your sacrifices, your tithes, and the heave offering of your hand, and all your choice vows which ye vow unto the Lord:

Psalm 103:7 described Moses as a person longing to know the ways of God, while Israel continually clamored for His acts. Did you ever wonder what it would have been like to gather manna in the morning during the moments when the pillar of fire transitioned into the cloud of daily covering? What was it like to drink the miracle water flowing from a solid rock? What about seeing the fire of God fall from heaven upon a sacrificial offering?

These things and many more were standard occurrences in the midst of a people regularly complaining about the provision of God. The acts of the hand of God were only as memorable as their last point of provision. What would He do today?

The Psalmist wrote of the manner through which Israel provoked the Almighty during the season of seeking the *m'nuwchah*. These people were the chosen of the Lord God and embraced by the presence of God. His cloud and pillar were continually around them. His miracles were regularly known on their behalf. Yet, with all of the indications of the *nuwach*, they were not mature enough to embrace the promise of *m'nuwchah*.

Psalm 95:8-11 Harden not your heart, as in the provocation, and as in the day of temptation in the wilderness: [9] *When your fathers tempted me, proved me, and saw my work.* [10] *Forty years long was I grieved with this generation, and said, It is a people that do err in their heart, and they have not known my ways:* [11] *Unto whom I sware in my wrath that they should not enter into my rest.*

The modern church is also in love with the acts of God, but few long to know God in His ways. This type of approach will leave us prone to the "what have you done for me lately" syndrome. Jesus regularly asked about the motives of those coming to hear Him. Had they come to see a sign, or to learn of Him and the Heavenly Father? The church in our day is called to establish the Tabernacle of David. The heart of this Tabernacle is found in seeking the *m'nuwchah* of God.

The Heart of David and his Tabernacle

King David loved the heart of God. In the most famous of Psalms, David wrote of the still waters to which God would lead him. The still waters are literally the *m'nuwchah* waters.

Psalm 23:1-6 The Lord is my shepherd; I shall not want. [2] *He maketh me to lie down in green pastures: he leadeth me beside the still waters.* [3] *He restoreth my soul: he leadeth me in the paths of righteousness for his name's sake.* [4] *Yea, though I walk through the valley of the shadow of death, I will fear no evil: for thou art with me; thy rod and thy staff they comfort me.* [5] *Thou preparest a table before me in the presence of mine enemies: thou anointest my head with oil; my cup runneth over.* [6] *Surely goodness and mercy shall follow me all the days of my life: and I will dwell in the house of the Lord for ever.*

In the Twenty-third Psalm, a stream of water attends to the person dwelling in this place of continual provision and confidence. The Word identified the existence of many streams making glad the city of our God. Streams represent refreshing and fertility, as well as the prospect of travel and access. From this place of continued measure of the active presence and breath of God, there is a promise of paths of righteousness. These paths are ones of triumphant dominion in the name, or purpose of the Lord God.

Deep within the heart of the King, there existed an ever present desire to create the place of *m 'nuwach* for the nation. David enjoyed the presence of God, and he desired to make the Heart of God available to the people. This sentiment was a continual passion within him, and it reflected the burning desire within the Heart of the Heavenly Father.

While David had the Tabernacle with him, it was always in the Heart of the King to build a permanent house for the breath of God. This is the heart continually seeking after God, and not simply for the momentary delight of His presence. David wanted the Spirit of God, and he longed to establish the place of continual visitation with Him.

Psalm 132:8 Arise, O Lord, into thy rest; thou, and the ark of thy strength.

When simply considering this passage in our vernacular, without the benefit of an understanding of the meaning of m'nuwchah, this verse would appear confusing. How can someone rise to their rest?

The passage is particularly compelling when we consider the meaning of *m 'nuwchah*. God does arise with great anticipation to

49

the acceptance of His prepared place of m'nuwchah. This is a moment of excitement as opposed to one wherein weariness is addressed.

David and Solomon

The subject of why David was not permitted to build the Temple of God is a matter of great speculation and discussion. Of the myriad Scriptural passages speaking of this issue, God judged David to be more of a warrior than a man capable of settling into the place necessary to direct this process of *m'nuwchah*. David was judged to be a man of war with a propensity to shed blood.

> *1 Chronicles 28:2-3 Then David the king stood up upon his feet, and said, Hear me, my brethren, and my people: As for me, I had in mine heart to build an house of rest for the ark of the covenant of the Lord, and for the footstool of our God, and had made ready for the building: ³ But God said unto me, Thou shalt not build an house for my name, because thou hast been a man of war, and hast shed blood.*

The prohibition against David building the Temple is not an expression indicting God as a pacifist. The warfare of David was directed by God. The only lasting challenge God had with David was in his arranged murder of Uriah (I Kings 15:5). For this action, David was severely punished.

David specifically listed the reason he was excluded from building the Temple. He simply felt the need to be out and about in continued action, and was not inclined to successfully direct the supervision of the place of habitation. For David, the presence of God was an active measure of fellowship as he aggressively sought measures of conquest. His personal life was one of *m'nuwchah*, and he longed for this to be an existent factor for the nation itself.

Without the prospect of war and conquest, David was not fulfilled. This was where he found His Heavenly Father. When bereft of the excitement of subjugation, David was seemingly not fulfilled. In fact, being confined to Jerusalem during the time when Kings went forth to war was the factor leading to the great sin of King David. The murder of Uriah and the acquisition of Bathsheba was the result. Even in this, the love of God was shown. The son of David and Bathsheba would then build the Temple, or the place of *m'nuwchah*. This son would be the first in the heritage line of David eventually conceiving the Messiah.

The Pronouncement unto the Sons of David

To the sons of David, God promised an everlasting measure of *m'nuwchah*. This is particularly wonderful considering our Lord Jesus was born into the lineage of David. As the firstborn of many sons, Jesus ensured the opportunity for a redeemed people to avail themselves of this everlasting promise of the Heavenly Father. According to the Book of Hebrews, our Mt. Zion is in Heaven. We have every right and privilege to enjoy the measure of *m'nuwchah*.

Psalm 132: 11-18 The Lord hath sworn in truth unto David; he will not turn from it; of the fruit of thy body will I set upon thy throne. ¹² If thy children will keep my covenant and my testimony that I shall teach them, their children shall also sit upon thy throne for evermore. ¹³ For the Lord hath chosen Zion; he hath desired it for his habitation. ¹⁴ This is my rest for ever: here will I dwell; for I have desired it. [15] *I will abundantly bless her provision: I will satisfy her poor with bread.* [16] *I will also clothe her priests with salvation: and her saints shall shout aloud for joy.* [17] *There will I make the horn of David to bud: I have ordained a lamp for mine anointed.* [18] *His enemies will I clothe with shame: but upon himself shall his crown flourish.*

Solomon was commissioned to build and welcome the continual place of *m'nuwchah*. He followed the vision of his earthly father, and welcomed the wisdom of his Heavenly Father. The pronouncement of David upon Solomon is profound. Can you imagine the Heavenly Father pronouncing these words of promise over you? You should, for the Almighty is saying them at this very moment.

1 Chronicles 22:6-13 Then he called for Solomon his son, and charged him to build an house for the Lord God of Israel. [7] *And David said to Solomon, My son, as for me, it was in my mind to build an house unto the name of the Lord my God:* [8] *But the word of the Lord came to me, saying, Thou hast shed blood abundantly, and hast made great wars: thou shalt not build an house unto my name, because thou hast shed much blood upon the earth in my sight.* [9] *Behold, a son shall be born to thee, who shall be a man of rest; and I will give him rest (nuwach) from all his enemies round about: for his name shall be Solomon, and I will give peace and quietness unto Israel in his days.* [10] *He shall build an house for my name; and he shall be my son, and I will be his father; and I will establish the throne of his kingdom over Israel for ever.* [11] *Now, my son, the Lord be with thee; and prosper thou, and build the house of the Lord thy God, as he hath said of thee.* [12] *Only the Lord give thee wisdom and understanding, and give thee charge* concerning Israel, that thou mayest keep the law of the Lord thy God. *[13]* Then shalt thou prosper, if thou takest heed to fulfil the statutes and judgments which the Lord charged Moses with concerning Israel: be strong, and of good courage; dread not, nor be dismayed.

Read the dedicatory words Solomon spoke over the newly completed Temple in Jerusalem. Shortly after these words were spoken, the very tangible presence of God fell upon the Temple and the people. The days of this type of visitation are soon to touch the earth again.

1 Kings 8:54-61 And it was so, that when Solomon had made an end of praying all this prayer and supplication unto the Lord, he arose from before the altar of the Lord, from kneeling on his knees with his hands spread up to heaven. [55] And he stood, and blessed all the congregation of Israel with a loud voice, saying, [56] Blessed be the Lord, that hath given rest unto his people Israel, according to all that he promised: there hath not failed one word of all his good promise, which he promised by the hand of Moses his servant. [57] The Lord our God be with us, as he was with our fathers: let him not leave us, nor forsake us: [58] That he may incline our hearts unto him, to walk in all his ways, and to keep his commandments, and his statutes, and his judgments, which he commanded our fathers. [59] And let these my words, wherewith I have made supplication before the Lord, be nigh unto the Lord our God day and night, that he maintain the cause of his servant, and the cause of his people Israel at all times, as the matter shall require: [60] That all the people of the earth may know that the Lord is God, and that there is none else. [61] Let your heart therefore be perfect with the Lord our God, to walk in his statutes, and to keep his commandments, as at this day.

In Isaiah 6, Isaiah experienced the attending presence of God as He showed Himself within this very Temple. This is the same God that exists with us today, and it is His intent to similarly visit us with His presence and power. There was not an Old Testament God and a New Testament God, for He is one in the same. If He would transact the following visitation with Isaiah, He will certainly do so with us.

Isaiah 6:1 In the year that king Uzziah died I saw also the Lord sitting upon a throne, high and lifted up, and his train filled the temple.

The train of the Lord God is the hem of His garment. What a marvelous scene of triumph. This is the prospect of the place where God will dwell with us. The scenes of angelic visitation and the impartation of divine anointing are awesome to behold. It is what God intends for the place of His rest in our day.

What is the post-script of the earthly Temple of Solomon? In Isaiah 66, long after the days of Solomon and long after the visitation Isaiah experienced in the Temple, we find the intent of God was the same as it had been during the days before the Temple was built.

Isaiah 66:1-2 Thus saith the Lord, The heaven is my throne, and the earth is my footstool: where is the house that ye build unto me? And where is the place of my rest? ² For all those things hath mine hand made, and all those things have been, saith the Lord: but to this man will I look, even to him that is poor and of a contrite spirit, and trembleth at my word.

The place of the *m'nuwchah* of God is not made of brick, precious stone and metal. It is formed through the men and women obeying God, accepting His direction and welcoming His presence. From the earthly Temple, the cry of God through Isaiah speaks to those contrite and desirous of the Most High. The people to whom Isaiah initially wrote did not heed this call. They were subsequently conquered and dispersed into the captivity of serving other nations.

The words of Micah echo to us the result of this tragic loss of purpose. As you read the following verses, can you feel the desperation of the Most High for His place of continued dwelling among them? Because the people did not seek after God, they were thrown into disarray and defeat. In verse 10, God told these people a dismal and iniquitous existence was not His plan for them, as this was not the *m'nuwchah.*

Micah 2:4-11 In that day shall one take up a parable against you, and lament with a doleful lamentation, and say, We be utterly spoiled: he hath changed the portion of my people: how hath he removed it from me! turning away he hath divided our fields. [5] Therefore thou shalt have none that shall cast a cord by lot in the congregation of the Lord. [6] Prophesy ye not, say they to them that prophesy: they shall not prophesy to them, that they shall not take shame. [7] O thou that art named the house of Jacob, is the spirit of the Lord straitened? are these his doings? do not my words do good to him that walketh uprightly? [8] Even of late my people is risen up as an enemy: ye pull off the robe with the garment from them that pass by securely as men averse from war. [9] The women of my people have ye cast out from their pleasant houses; from their children have ye taken away my glory for ever. [10] Arise ye, and depart; for this is not your rest: because it is polluted, it shall destroy you, even with a sore destruction. [11] If a man walking in the spirit and falsehood do lie, saying, I will prophesy unto thee of wine and of strong drink; he shall even be the prophet of this people.

The Pattern for the People of God

In our day, God offers His point of blessing and abundance. Divine wisdom as was granted to Solomon is necessary for the people of God as they welcome sonship. From this embracing of the purpose of God there is an empowerment of blessing and provision.

The Spirit of Wisdom and Revelation will be afforded to the sons of God as they pursue the provision of His dwelling place. According to Isaiah 11, the *nuwach* of God will accomplish this impartation of wisdom. Righteousness will abundantly be poured out upon the land of heritage. And, in verse 10, we perceive upon the lineage of David the glorious *m'nuwchah* soon to be witnessed by the entire Gentile world.

Isaiah 11:1-10 And there shall come forth a rod out of the stem of Jesse, and a Branch shall grow out of his roots: [2] *And the spirit of the Lord shall rest (nuwach) upon him, the spirit of wisdom and understanding, the spirit of counsel and might, the spirit of knowledge and of the fear of the Lord;* [3] *And shall make him of quick understanding in the fear of the Lord: and he shall not judge after the sight of his eyes, neither reprove after the hearing of his ears:* [4] *But with righteousness shall he judge the poor, and reprove with equity for the meek of the earth: and he shall smite the earth with the rod of his mouth, and with the breath of his lips shall he slay the wicked.* [5] *And righteousness shall be the girdle of his loins, and faithfulness the girdle of his reins.* [6] *The wolf also shall dwell with the lamb, and the leopard shall lie down with the kid; and the calf and the young lion and the fatling together; and a little child* shall lead them. *⁷ And the cow and the bear shall feed; their young ones shall lie down together: and the lion shall eat straw like the ox. ⁸ And the sucking child shall play on the hole of the asp, and the weaned child shall put his hand on the cockatrice' den. ⁹ They shall not hurt nor destroy in all my holy mountain: for the earth shall be full of the knowledge of the Lord, as the waters cover the sea. ¹⁰ And in that day there shall be a root of Jesse, which shall stand for an ensign of the people; to it shall the Gentiles seek: and his rest (m'nuwchah) shall be glorious.*

The Wisdom of Issachar

Of the Tribes of Israel, Issachar most readily perceived the benefit and necessity of *m'nuwchah*. Issachar was the group possessing wisdom and the knowledge of the mind of the Lord God for Israel. Understanding the times, this tribe was classified in Genesis 49 as having been positioned between two burdens.

Genesis 49:13-18 Zebulun shall dwell at the haven of the sea; and he shall be for an haven of ships; and his border shall be unto Zidon. ¹⁴ Issachar is a strong ass couching down between two burdens: ¹⁵ And he saw that rest was good, and the land that it was pleasant; and bowed his shoulder to bear, and became a servant unto tribute. ¹⁶ Dan shall judge his people, as one of the tribes of Israel. ¹⁷ Dan shall be a serpent by the way, an adder in the path, that biteth the horse heels, so that his rider shall fall backward. ¹⁸ I have waited for thy salvation, O Lord.

For Issachar to recognize the *m'nuwchah* as being "good" is something quite profound. The word translated as good in this verse is the Hebrew word *towb*, the good of the Tree of the

Knowledge of Good and Evil. *Towb* is the embraced and applied purpose of God. Issachar recognized the purpose of God is to realize His active and attendant breath.

The wise tribe of Issachar was mentioned between the warrior tribe of Zebulun and the judges of Dan. These could be the identity of the two burdens, as they represent the assessment and application of the people of God. It is always a burden to convince people to accept and apply this pure message of divine purpose.

The burden of Issachar might also be a depiction of the positioning between heaven and earth, light and dark. The sons of God represent Him before people and before the spirit realm. Being in the midst of the church, in the midst of the enemy, and in the midst of purpose and iniquity is the place where the sons are situated.

Issachar was additionally responsible to deal with an equal burden between seasons and times, comprising a balance connecting the right side of prophetic understanding and the left side of activation and fulfillment of promise.

Will we welcome the ultimate desire of the Lord to this earth? We are called to embrace Him to the degree His will might be done on earth as it is in heaven. Sons will be sent from this place of *m'nuwchah* to accomplish the will of God in the surrounding territory.

As mentioned at the beginning of this chapter, *m'nuwchah* is in the feminine gender. *M'nuwchah* will welcome the Sabaoth seed of the purpose of God, and produce His will upon the earth. The masculine of this Hebrew word is *manowach*, and it portrays the going forth of the sons of heritage, the seed of David, from the point of the presence of the Almighty.

It makes sense that there would not solely be a place of fertility without an offspring from that fertility. For every *m'nuwchah* there should be the offspring of champions of *manowach.*

The Father of Samson

Manoah is a transliteration of *manowach.* In the Book of Judges, a man by this name was the father of Samson, the great judge of Israel that withstood the Philistines. Through a miraculous birth, Manoah and his wife were able to bring the baby Samson into the world. His life would wreak havoc amongst the enemy forces bent on withstanding the blessings of the children of God in their promised land.

What a phenomenal picture of the desire of God upon and through the place where His glorious breath is enthroned! Samson was born into the tribe of Dan, one of the tribes flanking Issachar.

The Bible detailed the *ruwach* of the Lord as prodding and stirring Samson when he was a boy. This was as a means of training Samson to move in the obedience and in the power of the Spirit.

Judges 13:25 And the Spirit of the Lord began to move him at times in the camp of Dan between Zorah (screech, shout loudly) and Eshtaol (demand, make an earnest appeal).

Perhaps the breath of God is prodding you in this hour. Maybe He is stirring up the prophetic import of words spoken over your life. There are words laying dormant within your heart that God wants to activate at this time in delivering power.

The names of the two cities mentioned in the above verse provide an insight in themselves. As we combine the two parenthesized meanings of the cities, we understand it is our obligation to make an earnest and loud appeal before the Lord on behalf of His purpose. This shout of delight is a picture of the breath of God as it flows through us.

Chapter 4

Ruwah

In this day, judges are being raised to impart the Spirit of God into His creation. Just as in the time of Samson, the Spirit of God is moving His people to shout an earnest appeal concerning the vital requests of righteousness.

God desires we recognize the importance and power of our words. The spoken sound is vital, as everything begins with a voice. Prophetic enunciations are of great importance to the people of God. Our expressions from the breath of our lips are expressions of the life-flow within us. He also wants us to recognize there is power in our shout.

There is a powerful expression known as the shout of the Lord. This shout can express the exaltation and exuberance of the delight and confidence of the Lord. It can be a devastating weapon in a moment of warfare. Both of these exhibitions of the shout stem from the Hebrew word *ruwah*, a derivative of *ruwach*. In essence, when we apply the shout of the Lord, we are expressing a demonstration of the very nature of God.

Ruwah means the sound of joy or the breaking of the ear by the enunciation of delight and triumph. Mankind was not the first of the creation of God to utter this type of enthusiastic cry. The angels were the first to release this type of vocalization.

Job 38:7 When the morning stars sang together, and all the sons of God shouted for joy?

God Himself emits this magnificent type of shout whenever he goes forth as a man of war. Not only does the Word tell us the Almighty will shout, but there is also a roar proceeding from the mouth of God. Whether this is the roar of the Lion of Judah, or not, it is truly a roar of cataclysmic proportion.

Isaiah 42:13 The Lord shall go forth as a mighty man, he shall stir up jealousy like a man of war: he shall cry, yea, roar (a very clear and loud cry); he shall prevail against his enemies.

Although it is a New Testament passage, the heavenly shout occurring at the rapture of the church will be of this same variety (I Thessalonians 4:16). When the Day of the Lord approaches, a *ruah* will be offered in the holy mountain of God.

Joel 2:1 Blow ye the trumpet in Zion, and sound an alarm in my holy mountain: let all the inhabitants of the land tremble: for the day of the Lord cometh, for it is nigh at hand;

The shout is to be an ongoing expression within the repertoire of the people of God. In some churches, clapping of the hands is an accepted mode of worshipful expression. If we recognize this offering of praise, we must also allow for the accompanying shout of the Lord.

Psalm 47:1 To the chief Musician, A Psalm for the sons of Korah. O clap your hands, all ye people; shout unto God with the voice of triumph

In Preparation for warfare

It would appear the shout of the Lord elicits a release of affinity and power on behalf of the people of God. Whenever the people of God are engaged in righteous purpose, and they utter the *ruwah*, the hand of the Lord will intervene and bring a strong measure of confidence and assurance.

> *Numbers 10:9 And if ye go to war in your land against the enemy that oppresseth you, then ye shall blow an alarm with the trumpets; and ye shall be remembered before the Lord your God, and ye shall be saved from your enemies.*

> *1 Samuel 17:20 And David rose up early in the morning, and left the sheep with a keeper, and took, and went, as Jesse had commanded him; and he came to the trench, as the host was going forth to the fight, and shouted for the battle.*

> *1 Samuel 17:52 And the men of Israel and of Judah arose, and shouted, and pursued the Philistines, until thou come to the valley, and to the gates of Ekron. And the wounded of the Philistines fell down by the way to Shaaraim, even unto Gath, and unto Ekron.*

In each of the three previous instances, when the *ruwah* of the people of God was released, it set in motion a vital measure of the victorious presence of God, even before a weapon was raised in battle. David spoke of the favor of this kind of agreement before the Lord when he proclaimed the enemy does not have this measure of weaponry at his disposal.

> *Psalm 41:11 By this I know that thou favourest me, because mine enemy doth not triumph over me.*

The *ruwah* would appear to be the sound raised prior to the battle itself. The *ruwah* is an exaltation of the presence of the Lord among the people, declaring He is in favor with their righteous cause. The *t'ruwah* is the launching of favor in physical or spiritual battle. This battle cry is in reality an applied *ruwah*.

How do we recognize the difference between the *ruwah* and the *t'ruwah*, seeing they are extensions of the *ruwach* of God? Although the lines of distinguishing might be blurry at times, there is a simple rule to ascertain one from the other. The *ruwah* occurs within the camp as a celebration of the majesty of God. The *t'ruwah* is associated with battle. A congregation or a prayer group must rely upon the wisdom of God and the directive of leadership in order to properly apply an assignment of usage.

These concepts are echoed in the storied behavior of many cultures throughout the history of mankind. Think of some of them with me. In the traditions of the American Indian tribes, we hear of the campfire songs that told of bravery in battle. Songs sung within the camp included those focusing upon warfare, and many were dedicated to a devoted dependence upon supernatural forces for assistance in the coming day of conflict. This would be a type of the *ruwah* in their midst. Everyone knows of the blood-curdling, battle cry of the Indian warrior. Through the war "whoop," a type of *t'ruwah* is seen. The battle cry inspired confidence within the warrior, and instituted fear in the souls of the opponent.

Many cultures and nations can espouse illustrations similar to this one from the lore of the American Indian. Something deep within mankind feels the need and power to exhibit these types of expressions.

Within the pages of the history of the United States, we readily see this same type of release of sound. During the American Civil War, the Confederate forces would sing songs around the tent fires at night. These melodies would galvanize the soldier with thoughts of home and of their devotion to what they believed was their reason for being engaged in warfare. Who has not heard stories of the infamous "rebel yell" that was heard upon countless battlefields. Years after the end of the conflict, at a reunion of soldiers from both North and South, a Confederate veteran was asked to release an example of the famed battlefield cry. He said that it could not be done, for it only could be shown in the heat of battle.

God wants His people to capture the vigor of ruah and t'ruwah, for they are divinely placed within the heart of man in order to be used for the Glory of God. Examples of the divine impulse of God-given shouting are readily found through the Bible.

Examples of ruwah and t'ruwah

When Joshua and the children of Israel marched in silence around the walls of Jericho, they were obediently preparing for the mighty power of God to be exhibited in a magnificent manner. The people were instructed to lift a *ruwah*, followed by a *t'ruwah*. The result was the miraculous destruction of the great walls of Jericho.

> *Joshua 6:5 And it shall come to pass, that when they make a long blast with the ram's horn, and when ye hear the sound of the trumpet, all the people shall shout (ruwah) with a great shout (t'ruwah); and the wall of the city shall fall down flat, and the people shall ascend up every man straight before him.*

In the days of Eli, when Samuel was just a young man, there occurred a negative example of the way warfare should be conducted. The shout does not function in an independent manner bereft of the directive of the Lord. Sometimes people will attempt to use the weapons or principles of the Lord in an effort to conduct their own wishes and desires.

When battle against the Philistines had gone awry, the people reasoned they should fetch the Ark of the Covenant from Shiloh. When it was brought into the camp, the people of Israel offered up the *ruwah* and then the *t'ruwah*. The problem with this strategy was God had not directed these actions.

Interestingly, the Philistines were well aware of the *ruwah* and of the Ark of the Covenant. Their recorded conversation in regard to this perception was quite revealing. The combination of this release of the shout along with the presence of the Ark of the Covenant brought fear into the enemy camp. Since God had not directed Israel in this battle, and not only were the people of God defeated but the Ark was temporarily in Philistine hands.

1 Samuel 4:5 And when the ark of the covenant of the Lord came into the camp, all Israel shouted (ruwah) with a great shout (t'ruwah), so that the earth rang again.

For an insufferably long time, the Ark of the Covenant was displaced from its intended point of worship. God used this period of unsettledness to prepare the fullness of what He had intended regarding the *m'nuwchah*. Although the Temple was years away from being constructed, God deemed it was time for the Ark of the Covenant to be brought into the Holy City.

King David was commissioned of God to bring the Ark of the Covenant into Jerusalem. On the pathway of this righteous action there was a hearty submission of praise on all manner of instruments. Sacrifices unto God were offered all along the corridor toward Jerusalem. In the midst of this spectacle of worship, the people lifted up the *t'ruwah*. Once again, this was a release of some type of warfare released into the invisible realm, and the entire earth "rang" as a result.

Why would the earth ring? According to Romans 8:19, creation displays an "earnest expectation" for the manifestation of the sons of God. As the Ark was being brought into Jerusalem in what would serve as the pattern of the installation of the *m'nuwchah* around the world, the earth rang with excitement. The *t'ruwah* was released to indicate this was a warfare march. The dwelling place of the Lord will be welcomed all over the world, and this march was indicative of what will happen throughout the footstool of the Lord.

2 Samuel 6:15 So David and all the house of Israel brought up the ark of the Lord with shouting, and with the sound of the trumpet.

During the days of the rebuilding of Jerusalem following Babylonian captivity, the people of God experienced a great deal of spiritual warfare. The opening of the timetable of the regathering of the people of God to Jerusalem was accomplished through the prayers and spiritual interventions of men like Daniel and Ezekiel.

When it came time for the remnant returning to Jerusalem to construct the foundation of the Temple, there was a great offering of specified praise before the Lord. The people presented a *ruwah* of triumphant devotion to God followed by the *t'ruwah*.

Ezra 3:11-13 (Days of Zerubbabel) And they sang together by course in praising and giving thanks unto the Lord; because he is good, for his mercy endureth for ever toward Israel. And all the people shouted (ruwah) with a great shout (t'ruwah) when they praised the Lord, because the foundation of the house of the Lord was laid. [12] *But many of the priests and Levites and chief of the fathers, who were ancient men, that had seen the first house, when the foundation of this house was laid before their eyes, wept with a loud voice; and many shouted (t'ruwah) aloud for joy:* [13] *So that the people could not discern the noise of the shout (t'ruwah) of joy from the noise of the weeping of the people: for the people shouted (ruwah) with a loud shout (t'ruwah) and the noise was heard afar off.*

What a dynamic articulation of heartfelt devotion to God! Who is to say what was released during the expression of *t'ruwah*. One thing is certain: we readily behold some measure of warfare was being conducted on behalf of the purpose of God at the site of the Temple.

Musical Expression of the t'ruwah

During the days of my upbringing, the church I attended would sing a song comprised from the following verse of Scripture. Little did we know the word translated as "joyful sound" is actually *t'ruwah*.

Psalm 89:15 *Blessed is the people that know the joyful sound: they shall walk, O Lord, in the light of thy countenance.*

Singing this chorus over the years was fun, but it was hardly a genuine expression of what God intended by the placement of the word for warfare shout. In our simplicity, we thought God wanted us to make delightful noises because we were so very happy. Even minimal points of obedience often had to be coerced through the insistence of leadership.

The people are supposed to offer up the shout of defined and well-placed warfare praise. The promise of the Lord is that as we lift up this warfare shout, blessing will be the result. Not only will we make the sound with our voices, but we are to play it upon instruments as we sing.

Psalm 33:3 Sing unto him a new song; play skilfully with a loud noise.

The instruments are also to play creatively and prophetically in warfare mode. A new song or a continually creative song is something that is insisted upon by the Most High. This is most likely the spiritual song that is commanded in Ephesians 5:19 and Colossians 3:16.

God must help His church to become less interested in performance and entertainment, and more focused upon creative worship. The enemy loves for the church to be robbed of warfare in worship, and he absolutely enjoys the rote approach of modern music. Uzzah was killed for trying to steady the Ark of the Covenant. It had been placed upon a new cart made of boards and big wheels. Most churches try to welcome the presence of God with the same approach. The results are the same, as everything might be made well and appear impressive, but the consequence is death.

The "selah of the silver trumpets" is listed in Psalm 47. A selah is a form of musical and intercessory expression wherein the people of God make a prophetic statement and then war through until the resolution of fulfillment arrives.

Psalm 47:5 God is gone up with a shout, the Lord with the sound of a trumpet.

When the worship was accepted by the Lord it was punctuated through the *t'ruwah,* or warfare shouts, that God accepted the sacrifice. The translation allows for God to flow through such a sound, or to utter it Himself. Perhaps both of these occurred at the same moment in time. The point is that some measure of victory was accomplished in the midst of this triumphant expression.

God loves the *t'ruwah* so much He commanded it to be offered in the last chapter of the Psalms.

Psalm 150:5 Praise him upon the loud cymbals: praise him upon the high sounding cymbals.

This instrumental offering of the *t'ruwah* was accomplished on the cymbals. These are loud. Most churches in western civilization are pacifists with sensitive ears and frayed nerves. God commands this deafening display to be offered by us, and we must seriously consider the meaning of His ordinance in our lives and in our churches.

The verse following this instruction of *t'ruwah* proclaims everything with *n'shammah* must praise the Lord. Obviously, the *t'ruwah* is for use wherever the air of life is breathed.

Moses instituted a Sabbath, or gathering of the sons, wherein there was to be a solemn *t'ruwah* of trumpets on the first day of the seventh month.

Leviticus 23:24 Speak unto the children of Israel, saying, In the seventh month, in the first day of the month, shall ye have a sabbath, a memorial of blowing_of trumpets, an holy convocation.

This is a hallmark of those with true authority in the spirit realm. The first day of the seventh month speaks of the idea of empowerment for some measure of commissioning. The sons gather on the seventh day to consider the conquest of the week to come. The first day of the seventh month might represent the release of dominion through the sons during the remaining part of the year. Perhaps this is something the church should incorporate within the modern calendar of ministry.

Earlier in this chapter, we cited Isaiah 42:13 wherein God offered up a *ruwah* in preparation for warfare. We conclude this chapter with a pronouncement of God as He offered up a *t'ruwah*.

Numbers 23:21 *He hath not beheld iniquity in Jacob, neither hath he seen perverseness in Israel: the Lord his God is with him, and the shout of a king is among them.*

The shout of the King and the shout of the sons is shown as being offered in unison upon the face of creation. The shout of the people of God welcomes the blessing of God in natural and spiritual environs. This is the shout echoing the breath of the nature of God.

Our shout of *ruwah* and *t'ruwah* is the very expression of the person of God within us, without our camp and throughout the field of righteous conquest. This is the theme of the Old Covenant and the New, for it is the sound of the breath of God resonating within our spirit.

71

Chapter 5

Breath of the New Covenant

As we have seen in our discussions throughout this book, the Lord God strongly desires for us to partner with Him in what He is doing in the world today. This partnership consists of our becoming like Him, and submitting ourselves to the chastening and refinement of sonship.

Partnering with God is not simply the acceptance of good ideas. It does not entail a mere commitment to a cause or a unified effort with others of like faith and values. To partner with God does not even imply you feel good about yourself with a strong sense of individual accomplishment. Pleasing God must be something we do for the sole purpose of gratifying and delighting Him.

This is why the long progression of understanding regarding His Spirit in the Old Testament embodies our becoming like Him. We are to embody His presence while we look for the places wherein He desires to establish His Kingdom in demonstrable fashion. Throughout the past two centuries, this kind of commentary would be considered a foolhardy and unscriptural concept within much of the church world.

Our emphasis has perennially been one of bringing people into a saving knowledge of the Lord Jesus Christ. Nobody would argue this is the most incredible miracle happening in this life. Where would we be without being born again? There would be no hope whatsoever in this life, or the next.

Churches resemble a family continuing to grow, but never encouraging their children to learn or get a job in order to apply themselves to meaningful employ. What would we say of a family only emphasizing the need to have more children? What would our opinion be of a family feeling that it knew everything while waiting for a climactic event to happen, while at the same time having as many babies as possible? Of course, this is ludicrous.

This is an extreme illustration, but there is a stark resemblance to the modern church readily seen in the midst of this preposterous scenario. The church is told to keep on bringing babies into the Kingdom while we await the rapture. We train the siblings, or brothers and sisters, to simply care for one another. We encourage the people to reproduce.

All the while, the earth is going to hell and will soon encounter destruction. It does not matter to the redeemed since, it is assumed, we will all be evacuated by the second coming before things really get bad. I grew up in the church, so I know the rhetoric. Does it sound familiar?

Can we serve the earth from the travesties described in the apocalyptic passages of the Word of God? No, we would never dare assume the Word could be changed. How does the destruction occur? There will be a major battle for the Kingdom. Informed intercession and strategic prophetic activations are necessary and vital, being offered across the earth in this very day.

What is the necessity of this type of activity? God sent Abraham forth to possess the land. It was not just given to him by the sovereign will of God. God told the children of promise that He would not give the land to them all at once, but they would partner with Him to take it. If God was simply going to destroy the enemy and drive him from the earth, why has He not done it before now? God does all things according to perfect plan, and will accomplish the redemption of His land through His sons.

The Gospel of the Kingdom

What topics did Jesus teach in the years before the Cross? As the disciples were sent out by the Lord Jesus prior to Calvary, what did they preach and teach? There is such a thing as the Gospel of the Kingdom and it is very much different from the Gospel of Grace. The Gospel of Grace is a saving message for mankind. The Gospel of the Kingdom is one of establishing the principles of God upon the earth.

Allow me to issue a special point of clarity here, lest a reader misinterprets my meaning. I am not suggesting the church is going to win so many spiritual victories upon this earth that we will create a utopian wonderland. The atrocities listed in the eschatological passages of the Bible cannot be avoided. The Bible is true, and will not change in any fashion.

As the Sons of God arise, there will be great opportunity for the hand of God to be shown in brilliant fashion upon the earth. Spiritual warfare will take center stage upon the face of civilization. Darkness will openly be confronted by the power of light. Magnificent signs of the visitation of the presence of God will be openly witnessed by mankind.

The battle lines are already drawn. Gross darkness will cover significant portions of the globe, while the light of God will shine brightly upon His people. As has been the case in the annals of the history of warfare, a retreating enemy force will often inflict great damage to the place from which it is evacuating. This will undoubtedly be the case in the days to come, as darkness is being pushed back according to the timetable of the Lord. When will the end come?

Matthew 24:14 And this gospel of the kingdom shall be preached in all the world for a witness unto all nations; and then shall the end come.

In the time of the end, the Gospel of the Kingdom will be pronounced all over the world. There will be great consternation at both the reception and rejection of this message. Subsequent points of empowerment will begin to manifest throughout the earth. We will perceive things absolutely destined to boggle the framework of what we have known to be an acceptable course of existence.

From the context of the above verse, the Kingdom of God will expand toward the fulfillment of the mystery of God. The operative word within this passage is the one translated as "witness." This is the word *marturion,* and it implies the laying down of life for a cause.

For many Christians, there is great confusion as to what is meant by laying down our life. In our world today, Christians interpret this command as meaning to lend their life, at times, for causes they deem worthy. For others, laying down the life means to integrate acceptably good teachings or experiences into our life without having to surrendering control to God. No matter which way it is sliced, to be a martyr means just what it says.

We cringe at the manner some religions have brought the idea of martyrdom to the center stage of terrorism. We hate the senseless destruction inflicted in the name of God. History is populated with martyrs to various causes and kingdoms. In WWII, the Japanese kamikazes were terrors to Allied soldiers and equipment, crashing their airplanes as guided torpedoes from the air. General Patton of the American Army said his soldiers should be less concerned about giving their lives for their country, and more determined to make the enemy give his life for his country. Great warfare quote aside, this is not the theme of spiritual warfare. Whoever loses his life for the sake of the Kingdom will find it.

Jesus taught about becoming violent concerning the things of the kingdom. This is not the violence of the brute force of extreme beliefs in the natural, but of the spirit realm.

Matthew 11:12 And from the days of John the Baptist until now the kingdom of heaven suffereth violence, and the violent take it by force.

The violence spoken here is a forcing out of one occupational force by another. The high places of the earth are objective strike points. The force implied is similar to the children's game "king of the hill." We must do whatever is necessary by the energy of devotion in order for God to triumph. Do you recall the course for victory listed in the Book of Revelation? To overcome something, there must be an exertion of force greater than what is being overcome.

Revelation 12:11 And they overcame him by the blood of the Lamb, and by the word of their testimony; and they loved not their lives unto the death.

The blood of the lamb and the *marturia* of commitment to the unchanging word of God is the way the church will defeat the enemy. What a concept! How foreign is this notion to much of the church world? As this prescription for Kingdom taking plays out across the globe, natural and supernatural acts will rock the face of humanity.

The objective of God remains the same. The *ruwach* desires for you to partner with Him versus the darkness. As you proceed under divine directives, the *nuwach* of God will inhabit your firstfruits offering. He will lead you into battle to establish the *m'nuwchah* throughout the earth.

The Saintly Breath

In the New Testament there is little distinction between one mention of the breath of the spirit and another. Typically, the Greek word *pneuma* is the word utilized to denote the breath or wind of God. Translated as either ghost or spirit in the King James Version of the Bible, there is a great measure of confusion amongst Christendom regarding the meaning of *pneuma*.

The regrettable translation of *pneuma* as ghost has led many to view the Spirit of God as some phantasm or an unpredictable will 'o the wisp type of entity. The New Testament should be interpreted in light of the Old. What we know of the Hebrew concept of the breath of God should help us to understand the changeless God throughout the New Testament.

When we apply what has been learned from the Old Testament regarding the breath of God, we can gain a clearer grasp of the more generic *pneuma* in the New Testament. The most prominent adjective for *pneuma* in the Greek New Testament is the word *hagios,* regularly translated as holy.

The word "holy" has become a euphemistic expression for just about anything religious. As a result of this continual mistreatment, the main facets of understanding that should accompany the word "holy" have become blurred in our modern thought processes.

The Greek word *hagios* speaks of the purpose or will of God. The angelic voices crying "Holy, Holy, Holy" before the Throne declare His mighty purpose soon to be revealed through His jealous zeal. To be "holy" is a statement proclaiming that you are purely focused upon the will of God. Holiness is a proactive pursuit of what God desires, making His passion your own. This is remarkably similar to what God spoke of in the way of firstfruits and *nuwach.*

Hagios is the word the angels proclaim before the Throne of God. It is also the name of a group of people the Bible calls the saints, a distinct collection of people differentiated in the Scriptures as a part of, but distinct from the general church. We are all called to be saints, just as we are given the power to become the sons of God.

John 1:12 But as many as received him, to them gave he power to become the sons of God, even to them that believe on his name:

Those receiving Jesus have a choice as to whether they will proceed in His power toward becoming a son of God.

The acceptance of this invitation is up to us, and our response will determine what type of servant we can become before the Almighty. The Apostle Paul spoke openly of varying degrees of service within the family. He grieved over the lack of depth in many. Jesus also displayed this same type of incredulity concerning the lack of development within His disciples. Being a child of God does not necessarily mean you are moving in the power of sonship.

When the *hagios pneuma* is spoken of in the Greek New Testament, we see the prospect of God empowering a people to accomplish His purpose. Wrongfully, we have limited this empowerment of the Holy Spirit to the Day of Pentecost outpouring of Acts 2. The undeniable testimony of Scripture indicates that this Holy Spirit was active in strategic manner within the people of God in the days of the Old Testament. Without the ministry of the Holy Spirit prior to Pentecost, that significant moment would not have occurred.

Instances of the Saintly Wind Prior to Pentecost

While the Day of Pentecost in the New Testament was a hallmark issuance of the gift from God to the church, the Holy Spirit is regularly identified as having operated within and upon a number of mighty people prior to Pentecost. God desires to empower you in the same manner as He equipped these mighty men and women of God. The saintly wind is powerfully operative today. In order to understand some of the ways this dimension of God moves, we must observe them in the lives of these people. Each one of them played a major role in preparing for the welcoming of *m'nuwchah* throughout creation.

- In the life of David

Jesus testified of the fact that King David wrote and prophesied under the auspices and empowerment of the Holy Ghost. Notice what David said under the anointing of the Holy Ghost.

Mark 12:36 For David himself said by the Holy Ghost, The Lord said to my Lord, Sit thou on my right hand, till I make thine enemies thy footstool.

God is interested in His footstool. He is interested in the development of the sons of His right hand. This is the mandate of the Holy Spirit, and is the necessary force of the Tabernacle of David in our world today.

- In the Conception of Jesus

The immaculate conception of the Lord Jesus within the body of the virgin Mary was accomplished by the influence of the Holy Ghost. I once heard a mighty man of God say Christians should be like Mary, for we should all be travailing to bring the anointed sons into the world. This is the message of the Holy Ghost.

Matthew 1:18, 20 Now the birth of Jesus Christ was on this wise: When as his mother Mary was espoused to Joseph, before they came together, she was found with child of the Holy Ghost... [20] *But while he thought on these things, behold, the angel of the Lord appeared unto him in a dream, saying, Joseph, thou son of David, fear not to take unto thee Mary thy wife: for that which is conceived in her is of the Holy Ghost.*

-In the body of Elisabeth

Elisabeth was the Mother of John the Baptist. This pregnancy was miraculous in itself, having come at an advanced age in the lives of both she and her husband. When her cousin, Mary, came to visit during the time when they were both with child, the Bible says Elisabeth became filled with the Holy Ghost. The result of this infilling was shown by the baby within her leaping in response.

Luke 1:41 And it came to pass, that, when Elisabeth heard the salutation of Mary, the babe leaped in her womb; and Elisabeth was filled with the Holy Ghost:

- In the life of Zacharias

When John the Baptist was born, his Father was filled with the Holy Ghost and prophesied. Zacharias had been silenced by a word from Gabriel immediately prior to the conception of John. His tongue was empowered to speak when the forerunner of Jesus was born.

Luke 1:67 And his father Zacharias was filled with the Holy Ghost, and prophesied, saying,

- Prophetic insight to Simeon

When Jesus was a small child, Mary and Joseph brought the baby Jesus to the Temple in Jerusalem. Upon their entrance, the three encountered an old man named Simeon who had been awaiting their arrival. In fact, he had been waiting for a number of years because the Holy Ghost had prophetically told him at some point during his lifetime he would see the Messiah. Simeon obeyed this prophetic insight, and had faithfully applied himself to watch for the glorious day. When this man saw the baby Jesus, he prophesied because the Holy Ghost was upon him.

Luke 2:25-26 And, behold, there was a man in Jerusalem, whose name was Simeon; and the same man was just and devout, waiting for the consolation of Israel: and the Holy Ghost was upon him. [26] And it was revealed unto him by the Holy Ghost, that he should not see death, before he had seen the Lord's Christ.

- Within the Lord Jesus

Before Jesus was led of the Spirit into the wilderness, the Bible said He was full of the Holy Ghost, or the saintly wind. Imagine the Son of God needing the empowerment of the Holy Ghost to accomplish His mission, and recognize how much we need Him in our lives and ministries.

Luke 4:1 And Jesus being full of the Holy Ghost returned from Jordan, and was led by the Spirit into the wilderness,

- Breathed upon the Disciples

After His resurrection from the dead, the Lord Jesus appeared to the disciples many times. On one prolific occasion, the Lord Jesus breathed upon them and told them to receive the Holy Ghost, or saintly wind. We cannot miss the significance of this dynamic impartation from our Lord Jesus.

John 20:22 And when he had said this, he breathed on them, and saith unto them, Receive ye the Holy Ghost:

At the risk of confusing you, allow me to cite another passage occurring a few days following the time when Jesus breathed on the disciples, commanding them to receive the Holy Ghost.

> *Acts 1:5, 8 For John truly baptized with water; but ye shall be baptized with the Holy Ghost not many days hence...* [8] *But ye shall receive power, after that the Holy Ghost is come upon you: and ye shall be witnesses unto me both in Jerusalem, and in all Judaea, and in Samaria, and unto the uttermost part of the earth.*

Of course, this pre-ascension command of the Lord Jesus was culminated by the spectacular infilling of the Holy Ghost coming upon the thousands in Jerusalem at Pentecost. While we are not privy to most of the teachings Jesus gave to His disciples in the period between the Resurrection and Ascension, He must have explained the things concerning the Spirit to His disciples. They asked no questions concerning what He said in Acts 1. The angels appearing to them insisted they immediately to go Jerusalem to do what they had been instructed to do.

The teaching Jesus gave to them obviously included a treatise on the promise mentioned in Joel 2, for Peter immediately affixed an association with the Old Testament prophecy when the following visited the disciples in the Upper Room and the thousands gathered in the surrounding streets.

> *Acts 2:4 And they were all filled with the Holy Ghost, and began to speak with other tongues, as the Spirit gave them utterance.*

What is the meaning of all of this? When was the Holy Ghost given, anyway? The Spirit of God was dynamically active within the Old Testament, as we have plainly seen in the studies we have shared together in this book.

It is obvious, from the perusal of the Scriptures cited in this chapter, the Holy Ghost has been active in the lives of people for thousands of years. There are also very clearly stated New Testament impartations of the Holy Spirit occurring during the days prior to Pentecost.

With this in mind, let us examine the meaning of why Jesus breathed upon the disciples so they might receive the Holy Ghost. Many are confused as to why the Lord Jesus would then tell them to go to Jerusalem and tarry for the Holy Ghost infilling?

The answer to this question is simple, in light of the course of our discussions regarding the ways the Spirit of God has visited mankind. The eternal purpose of God involves the development of sons, and the partnering with them to establish His will within creation. The Holy Spirit, or saintly wind, is granted to people willing to embrace a particular assignment of the purpose of God. Jesus breathed upon the disciples with a Holy Ghost anointing to tarry for the widespread outpouring of the Spirit of God upon the world.

This same spirit, according to Acts 2 and Joel 2, was first poured out upon all flesh. Then, sons and daughters are said to be the recipients of prophetic insight, dreams and visions. Finally, servants and handmaids were granted the opportunity of receiving a personal outpouring of the person of God through His *ruwach.*

Sonship is the governing principle of the New Testament. In anticipation of the birth of Jesus, people were miraculously anointed for the coming of the Son of God. Jesus came to the earth to provide the way for people to come into relationship with the Heavenly Father. His incarnation was surrounded by impartations of the Holy Spirit. Not only did our Lord obtain the opportunity of sonship but He also patterned the actions of a Son. The grand purpose of God in sonship was at stake during this point in time, and ancillary people to the cause were needful of the visitation of the saintly wind.

After the Cross, the Lord imparted an anointing of the saintly wind to the disciples so they could partner with God for the widespread release of this unction into the church and world. The promise of the loving Father was granted.

Progression of impartation is the manner of God. The *nuwach* through an Old Testament individual made a way for the establishment of the *m'nuwchah* wherein the breath of God could abide in the place of the location of divine choice. This is the same principle demonstrated in the New Covenant with the Saintly wind. God imparted to people so they could make a way for a greater measure of the indwelling of the Spirit. Pentecost was the release of the Holy Spirit on the birthday of the church.

The gift of the Holy Spirit has been classified in the Bible as being the Promise of the Father. Think about this with me for a moment. Was this really the promise of something the Father was going to give, since He had already given this to many prior to the Day of Pentecost? Or, was this promise one of Fatherhood to all of those accepting Him and His ways? The spirit of sonship was being given to the church, and the church was now being given the opportunity to be led of the Spirit, or breath of God.

Romans 8:14 For as many as are led by the Spirit of God, they are the sons of God.

Sons will partner with the spirit of God to accomplish the will of God. On the Day of Pentecost, unknown tongues were granted to the church. The Bible tells us whenever we speak in unknown tongues, we speak the mysteries of God.

1 Corinthians 14:2 For he that speaketh in an unknown tongue speaketh not unto men, but unto God: for no man understandeth him; howbeit in the spirit he speaketh mysteries.

Mysteries come in two forms in the New Testament, the *musterion* (segments of revelation) and the *apokalupsis* (the entirety of purpose). The Book of Revelation is literally The *Apokalupsis*, signifying it is the Book detailing the completion of the mystery of God. The word associated with tongues is *musterion*, and we are told this is what we are praying when we speak thusly.

Therefore, let him that speaks in unknown tongues pray, or commune with God. As we fellowship with God, the intercession will reveal increasing dimensions of the will and timing of God. Incremental points of revelation will be spoken to the people of intercession.

1 Corinthians 14:13 Wherefore let him that speaketh in an unknown tongue pray that he may interpret.

The beauty of this exchange allows for us to partner with God in capacities beyond our limited understanding. These tongues were symbolized as flames of fire, so they represent the Spirit of Judgment and Burning according to the mystery of His ways. This is a phenomenal blessing for all of us desirous of partnering with God as sons.

The Seven Spirits of God

Literally we are being permitted to function as representatives of the Throne of God. In the model prayer Jesus taught to His disciples, the first thing mentioned was the Holiness of our Heavenly Father. The prayer then proceeded to request the coming of the Kingdom of heaven and its establishment upon the earth.

You do recognize when Jesus taught the disciples to pray He focused upon the Kingdom coming to earth. This is our mandate of prayer. An Old Testament example of this type of heavenly intervention upon a person is found in the Book of Zechariah.

Zechariah 3:9 For behold the stone that I have laid before Joshua; upon one stone shall be seven eyes: behold, I will engrave the graving thereof, saith the Lord of hosts, and I will remove the iniquity of that land in one day.

When we read the powerful Book of Zechariah, it is apparent there was continued intervention of the heavens upon what was transpiring upon the earth. In this Old Testament story, we see the restoration of the place of *m'nuwchah* in operation before our very eyes.

The men representing God in this mission were functioning in the face of continued opposition from earthly and supernatural powers. Yet, God was mightily with Joshua, Zerubbabel and Zechariah. In the quoted verse, God gave to Joshua a stone with seven eyes upon it. According to the Book of Revelation, seven eyes are a representation of the seven Spirits of God.

Revelation 5:6 And I beheld, and, lo, in the midst of the throne and of the four beasts, and in the midst of the elders, stood a Lamb as it had been slain, having seven horns and

*seven eyes, which are the seven Spirits of God sent forth into
all the earth.*

Wait a second. How can there be seven Spirits of God? This
must be a misprint, or an errant translation. Certainly this has to
be some failure of the King James Version. Perhaps if you were
to look in a more modern paraphrase, in the linguistic
expressions of our day, it would certainly say something other
than seven Spirits.

I must inform you there really are seven Spirits of God and
they are seven dimensions of the breath of God. There are seven
expressions of the various capacities of His personality. There
are seven distinct demonstrations of the progression of His hand.
Consider two other passages from the Book of Revelation that
speak of the seven Spirits of God.

*Revelation 3:1 And unto the angel of the church in Sardis
write; These things saith he that hath the seven Spirits of God,
and the seven stars; I know thy works, that thou hast a name
that thou livest, and art dead.*

*Revelation 4:5 And out of the throne proceeded lightnings
and thunderings and voices: and there were seven lamps of fire
burning before the throne, which are the seven Spirits of God.*

Seven unmistakable variations of the breath of God are
spoken of as being seven lamps and seven eyes. On the surface,
and hearing it perhaps for the first time, this concept may appear
to be a bit confusing. However, this is really not a difficult thing
to understand. In the Old Testament, God revealed Himself
through the disclosure of seven specific names. Do seven diverse
names of God imply seven different Gods? No.

We have no problem understanding how we as human beings may at one moment be a spouse, a parent, an employee, a supervisor, an uncle or aunt, a son or daughter, a brother or sister.... the list goes on. While we might be all of those representations, we are one person. We can function within many levels and capacities, and yet maintain the integrity of our person. If we can do this, can we not accept the same diversity of the amazing God we serve? What is the identity of the seven Spirits of God?

When people think of the number seven, they regard it in many different ways. Seven is universally considered to be "lucky" by the people of the world. Christians also hold to the number with an almost certain awe, attributing perfection to it. God utilizes seven throughout His Word as a point of completion. In reality, seven is the manner through which God represents Himself, it being the signature of His name and identity.

God created the world in seven days. Each day of creative process aligns with the seven Spirits in dynamic fashion. There were seven feasts of Israel; every one of them bringing the people to fellowship with the God who loves them. Seven beatitudes tell of His desire that His children be just like Him. Sevens are everywhere in the word, but perhaps there is no more profound demonstration of the seven than in the signature of God filling the sky above us.

After the great flood had abated from the face of Mt. Ararat, God made a covenantal agreement with Noah concerning the earth. God placed His rainbow of seven colors in the sky as a covenant between mankind and Himself. To Noah, the man breathing after the ways of God for the earth, this demonstrable gift was an astounding token of the love of God for Him.

> *Genesis 9:13, 17 I do set my bow in the cloud, and it shall be for a token of a covenant between me and the earth:...* [17] *And God said unto Noah, This is the token of the covenant, which I have established between me and all flesh that is upon the earth.*

The rainbow is the signature of God declaring His covenant ownership of the earth. Consisting of seven colors, it has not altered in appearance or variation of pattern since the first day Noah witnessed it in the sky. There is much significance to these seven colors and their revealed pattern, particularly regarding His ways and purposes for creation. An understanding of their meaning will help us to better interpret the attribution of color in the Bible.

When revealed through the prism of light and water, the seven colors of the pattern of the Lord are witnessed. Within them, we readily behold the model of how the purpose of God manifests itself. Each of the colors is a showcase of one of the seven Spirits of God. The rainbow still shines in our sky and we have the opportunity to partner with God to accomplish all He wants to do on the earth. The eyes of the seven Spirits still look for a person willing to apply for the privilege of serving God in unfathomable dimension.

Rainbows will occur in a double helix, even though we regularly only see one of them. This is an indication God is reaching to us as we are reaching to Him, forming a magnificent partnership for the planet. There is wisdom in this fact, as well.

Will we see God in His fullness, or will we settle for what is easily perceived by virtue of what we know?

Many Christians will be afraid of such a discussion equating the seven Spirits of God and a rainbow. Their caution will be based upon their association with the rainbow as a symbol of some demonically driven organizations in the world today.

The New Age movement had often embraced the rainbow as an emblem of their pursuits of the spirit realm. Some homosexually based organizations also have chosen the rainbow as the symbol of their endeavors. While these are distasteful realities, these in themselves should not deter the believer from understanding the sign of covenant between God and the earth. The rainbow was issued by God in undeniable manner in His Word, and it shines brightly in every place where light penetrates moisture.

Even in the scholastic world, we can see the measure of attempted enemy intrusion into our understanding of the rainbow. If you were to visit a teacher-supply store, you would most likely discover that the reward stickers depicting a rainbow will conveniently leave out indigo blue, or the color representing the Spirit of Glory and of God. Most of these rainbows are shown as having six colors, indicating a decided humanistic bent.

A further consideration of the colors of the seven Spirits will be afforded by a review of the books entitled <u>The Seers Catalog</u> and the <u>Manual of the Seven Spirits</u>, available through Pneumatikos Publishing. For the sake of this writing, consider the handiwork of God as revealed in the rainbow of covenant. In the following chart, you can see the depictions of the seven Spirits and a configuration of them as they align with the colors of the rainbow.

Spirits of God

Revelation 1:4

John to the seven church which are in Asia: Grace be unto you, and peace from him which is and which was, and which is to come; to the seven Spirits which are before his throne;

COLOR OF RAINBOW	SPIRIT OF GOD	SCRIPTURE REFERENCE	APPLICATION	NAMES OF GOD	ARMOR OF LIGHT	OPPOSING DEMONIC ENTITY	CHARACTERISTIC SPIRITS
Red	Judgment & Burning	Isaiah 4:4 Isaiah 28:6	Alignment with God's Purpose *"Blessed are the poor in spirit"* *"Kingdom, power, glory forever"*	Jehovah Shalom (Peace) Sabaoth (Hosts)	Shoes of Preparation of Gospel of Peace	Leviathan	Unclean - Luke 4:32-33 Infirmity - Luke 13:11
Orange	Grace and Supplication	Zechariah 12:10 Hebrews 10:29	God's Promotion and Empowerment *"Blessed are they that mourn"* *"Deliver from evil"*	Jehovah Jireh (Provides)	Praying Always	Beelzebub	Man - Zeh 12:1 Jealousy - Num 5:14
Yellow	Wisdom & Revelation	Deut 4:9 Isaiah 11:2	Progressive Insight and Application *"Blessed are the meek"* *"Lead us, not into temptation"*	Jehovah Rohi (shephard)	Shield of Faith Sword of the Spirit	Prince of Power of Air	Slumber - Rom 11:8 Error - 1 John 4:6
Green	Prophecy, Life & Supply	Romans 8:2 Philippians 1:19 Revelation 9:10	Present Truth Rhema *"Blessed are they that hunger and thirst after righteousness"* *"Give us daily bread / forgiveness"*	Jehovah Rophe (Heals)	Helmet of the Hope of Salvation	Wormwood	Lying - 1 Kings 22:22 Divination - Acts 16:16
Blue	Holiness & Saintliness	Romans 1:4 Romans 8:15	Saintliness / Righteous Purpose *"Blessed are the merciful"* *"Thy Kingdom come, thy will be done"*	Jehovah Mekaddesh (Sanctifies)	Clothed with Humility Breastplace of Righteousness	Anti-Christ	1 John 4:3
Indigo	Glory of God	1 Peter 4:14	Glory of God / His Presence *(Deleted from wordly depiction)* *"Blessed are the pure in heart"* *"Hallowed be thy name"*	Jehovah Nissi (Banner) Shammah (God who is there)	Put on (enduo) Take unto you (anambulano)	Prince of this World	Bondage - Rom 8:15 Idolatry - Hosea 5:4
Violet	Truth & Sonship	John 14:17 2 Timothy 1:7	Sons of God / Royal Commission *"Blessed are the peacemakers"* *"Our Father in Heaven"*	Jehovah Tsidkenu (Righteousness)	Loins Girt about with Truth Cloak of Zeal	Behemoth	Seducing - 1 Tim 4:1 World - 1 Cor 2:12

Those studying light and color will attest to the fact that the spectrum of the rainbow is dependent upon the magnitude of light energy able to penetrate through the prism. A stronger factor of light is necessary to witness all seven colors in the sky, while a weaker power factor will only allow for the perception of several colors on the scale of seven as it proceeds from red.

If the rainbow were a meter, red would be the easiest color to depict. The energy waves of red appear in a large and unhurried pattern. At the other end of the spectrum is violet, requiring the highest volume of light energy in order to be seen. The energy waves of violet are quick, concise and condensed. Regardless of the intensity of light, the sequential progression of the colors in the rainbow remains the same and does not vary at all in succession.

When God signed His name in the sky above Noah and the Ark, this action said many things to us. For one, the man named *nuwach* was the touch point of the attendant breath of God in the earth. To him, God gave the covenant for His ways to be demonstrated upon the earth. The rainbow was a signature of covenant between God and mankind forever.

Genesis 9:12-14 And God said, This is the token of the covenant which I make between me and you and every living creature that is with you, for perpetual generations: [13] *I do set my bow in the cloud, and it shall be for a token of a covenant between me and the earth.* [14] *And it shall come to pass, when I bring a cloud over the earth, that the bow shall be seen in the cloud:*

As you read this passage, can you sense the incredible importance of this sign? What other continuing sight do we see in our world that reminds us so faithfully of the promise of God to His sons? The prism of color does not only fill the sky after a rain shower, but is also seen in the light as it shines through the water sprinkler in our lawn on a hot summers day. God is serious about His covenant for the earth, as His signature is witnessed in every country and in every place where the light meets the water of life.

A signature is placed upon something that is valuable, and something that has merit to our life. We understand this concept even from the earliest days of our memory. When I was a little boy, I wrote my name upon just about everything belonging to me. The article had my signature upon it in order to signify the object had meaning to me, and I owned it.

As I became older, I was asked to place my signature upon many types of documents. Some of these documents were promises stating I would make a certain number of payments on behalf of a purchase I was making. In some instances, my signature verifies I am in agreement with the statements upon a document. Whenever I sign a marriage license in my capacity as Pastor, I attest to the fact I have officially participated in a ceremony uniting a man and woman in matrimony. Wherever my signature was found, I was there. My name represented my life and person on the printed page from that day forward.

The signature of God is binding for eternity. When He signed His name upon the sky, He did so to forever affix His mark of ownership and commitment. Each of the seven colors defines His personality and presence to His footstool, the earth. His name signified a way for man to come to Him, and the mode from which man would proceed from the Throne of God to the earth.

When God looked over the earth in Genesis 1, He saw it was without form and void. This is a warfare term indicating the aftermath of carnage and destruction. The wind of God brooded over the face of the deep in response to the satanic rebellion. God said "Light," and since sound and light are on the same scientific wavelength, this meant there was both a measure of audible declaration and visible demonstration.

Likely there was a rainbow of color affirming the divine expression of ownership and creativity that spanned what had most recently been without form and void.. The next seven days of creation patterned a progressive demonstration of the seven Spirits of God. From this point, God began to instruct Adam and Eve concerning the ways of His wind.

The seven colors of the prism of the rainbow combine to form what is known as white light. This is the truth of God displayed in the fullness of His ways. John wrote that when Jesus came to the earth, it was as a light shining into the darkness. The very God who created all things was now shining His signature through the darkness, and the darkness could not overcome Him in His brilliance.

John 1:3-5 All things were made by him; and without him was not any thing made that was made. ⁴ In him was life; and the life was the light of men. ⁵ And the light shineth in darkness; and the darkness comprehended it not.

Jesus came so that we might have the light and life of fellowship with God. We are to be the sons of partnership with the heavenly Father, insisting upon the resting place of His presence within this earthly footstool.

The days of the end speak of the light of God coming upon His people while gross darkness encompasses the world. We are called to be covenant people with God on behalf of this earth. We must let our light shine before mankind so they will see our good works, and glorify our Father which is in heaven.

Chapter 6

Abba

The privilege of partnering with God is one of relationship with Him. We must always view the measure of fulfilling His will as a sacred duty, but we must never lose sight of the essential fact that this partnership must be based upon the passion of relationship with Him.

Moving within the wind, breath or Spirit of God is not an event or anomalous experience. It is not something we do, but rather something we are within our very being. Any person standing on a hillside can be blown by the wind. It is something entirely different to become a part of the wind itself. This is the essence of sonship.

In the Old Testament, the Hebrew word *ab* is a primitive word most readily translated as father. Listed as the first word in most Hebrew Lexicons, it would appear God wants us to recognize the concept of fatherhood at the very beginning of our understanding.

From this word *ab* are many strategic derivatives. For instance, the name Abraham is an extension of this root word for father. The mighty patriarch is classified in the Bible as being the Father of many nations and of those walking in faith. Other derivations of *ab* will all relate in some manner to the power of a father or leader.

Of these, the most intriguing is *abah*. This fantastic word means "to be acquiescent, to consent, to be willing and to breathe after or of." In modern Christian thought, the term *abah* is one commonly defined as an endearing term for a father. Perhaps the classification of "Daddy" is affixed to the understanding of the word. People have embraced this title as being one expressing thoughts of tenderness and sweet commune.

While it is not my intention to denigrate this particular understanding of the term *abah,* I must state unequivocally the idiom requires a much broader view and a more responsible place of endearment within the family. Literally, this word means to be so close to a father that you are breathing the same breath as he is.

In our relationship with God, whenever we call Him *abah* we are stating our relationship with Him is so close that we breathe His breath, embrace His passion and align with His heartbeat. We are the first to hear whatever comes from His lips, and our proximity to His ear would imply even the slightest whisper framed from our mouth would be heard.

Too often, we relegate the term *abah* to something we say when we are in trouble or when we are experiencing a particularly poignant moment with God. To desire this type of intimate relationship with God would require we breathe with Him all the time, and not just when we feel like it. This expression is one we utter in the midst of devotion to His purpose. Employed fifty times in the Old Testament, there is a strong sense of sonship effusing from each usage of *abah*.

Abah in the Land of Promise

The essence of sonship is relationship and partnering with God according to His purpose. We are to be engaged in the pursuit of the *towb* of foundational purpose. Adam was the prototype of this type of walk before God. Each day, the *ruwach* of God would come to visit with Adam. This was undoubtedly a fellowship setting, where God would relate with His creation, but there was much more to the time of meeting with God.

During these encounters, the presence of the Lord would instruct Adam regarding the Tree of the Knowledge of Good (*towb*) and Evil (*ra*). There was a continuing measure of instruction concerning how the purpose of God should be observed, as well as how iniquity could destroy the intended function of good.

Isaiah wrote if we would be *abah* and devoted to a precise application of the purpose of God, the towb of creation would manifest itself. This would be a blessing for the earth as well as for Adam and Eve.

Isaiah 1:19 If ye be willing and obedient, ye shall eat the good (towb) of the land:

If mankind chooses to breathe the breath of the Heavenly Father, and applies what is imparted through relationship with God, things will work marvelously well. If humanity refuses such a privilege, there will be destruction. The mouth or the blowing of the breath of God, proclaims this fact.

Isaiah 1:20 But if ye refuse and rebel, ye shall be devoured with the sword: for the mouth of the Lord hath spoken it.

This is quite a contract. In our study of *abah* in the Old and New Testaments, we discover the embodiment of the wind of God is a loving but exacting process of submission and devotion. Practically all of the references to *abah* within the Old Testament are those detailing the training of individuals to partner with God. Sadly, most of these instances indicate a decided rejection of the appeal of the Father. Reflect upon some of the examples of *abah* involving the training of the Lord.

Abah and the Training of the Lord God

The quintessential passage of the Old Testament speaking of the importance of other tongues, and the walk of the spirit-filled life, is Isaiah 28. Within this setting, God spoke through Isaiah that he offered a strong measure of partnering with His m'*nuwchah* to the ones called to *nuwach,* but the people would not *abah.*

Isaiah 28:12 To whom he said, This is the rest (m'nuwchah) wherewith ye may cause the weary to rest (nuwach); and this is the refreshing: yet they would not hear.

What an astounding combination of promises from God to His people. The verse immediately prior to this one speaks of the stammering lips and unknown tongues of the mystery and commune with God.

Let us paraphrase this passage in order to gain a clear perspective. God said He would speak to the people through unknown tongues detailing His mystery. He said this would be the function of the m'*nuwchah* through which he would abide. He had called the people to walk in His firstfruits breath, but they would not get close enough to Him to operate as a covenant son.

Not only would the people fail to respond to His abiding presence, they would also fail to honor the words of the written law.

Isaiah 30:9 That this is a rebellious people, lying children, children that will not hear the law of the Lord:

Again, Isaiah spoke the heart of God in compassionate appeal to the people. They refused His offer of salvation peace that would be included in the provision of the lifestyle of *abah*.

Isaiah 30:15 For thus saith the Lord God, the Holy One of Israel; In returning and rest shall ye be saved; in quietness and in confidence shall be your strength: and ye would not.

For King David, the word of the Lord spoke in a subjective fashion. While Isaiah spoke of partnership, in the law and in deliverance, David cut right to the heart of the issue. A rejection of *abah* was a refusal of God Himself.

Psalm 81:11 But my people would not hearken to my voice; and Israel would none of me.

Impurity

The tribe of Benjamin would not hearken to the breath of the Lord through the other tribes. Being highly influenced by a Belial spirit (Anti-Christ), the tribe of Benjamin refused to purge itself of an offensive measure of impurity. We must recognize the enemy does not desire we partner with the presence and Spirit of God.

Judges 20:13 Now therefore deliver us the men, the children of Belial, which are in Gibeah, that we may put them to death, and put away evil from Israel. But the children of Benjamin would not hearken to the voice of their brethren the children of Israel:

Disobedience

Saul received a direct word from God through the prophet Samuel concerning what should happen with the spoils of a military triumph. In his measure of disobedience, the King did not harken to what God had commanded. This partial point of compliance with the directives of God was branded a failure to exhibit *abah.*

1 Samuel 15:9 But Saul and the people spared Agag, and the best of the sheep, and of the oxen, and of the fatlings, and the lambs, and all that was good, and would not utterly destroy them: but every thing that was vile and refuse, that they destroyed utterly.

Spiritual Purity

When Israel was brought out of Egypt bondage, they refused to allow Egyptian bondage to be brought out of them. In essence, the Israelites were not inclined to partner with God, but continued to rely upon the false promises of demonic worship.

A modern review of this historic perspective is heinous from to our eyes, but similar reality is also an indictment upon the church today. Christendom exists in a demonic culture, while regularly allowing for a thinly veiled reliance upon the demonic.

Ezekiel 20:8 But they rebelled against me, and would not hearken unto me: they did not every man cast away the abominations of their eyes, neither did they forsake the idols of Egypt: then I said, I will pour out my fury upon them to accomplish my anger against them in the midst of the land of Egypt.

Respecting the Anointed

God thinks so highly of those partnering with Him that He emphatically insists upon the respect due to them. In modern churches, there is not such respect for the truly anointed men and women of God serving Him. This topic could be addressed for many pages, but suffice God knows who belongs to Him. The laws of the *abah* are still intact.

- Doeg the Edomite

One of the vile compatriots of Saul, an Edomite named Doeg, held no such scruples of fear for the decrees of God as he deliberately murdered the priests of Nob. In an atrocious display, King Saul wanted these priests eliminated because they had helped David and his men to flee from his pursuit. None of the other soldiers of Saul would comply with his unrighteous command to kill the priests, except for Doeg. Anyone with reasonable intelligence and a passing understanding of Scripture would not act disrespectfully to those upon whom the hand of God rests.

- David

This is a test of whether someone is really operating in obedience to the Father. David, despite ready opportunity and warranted cause, displayed a hearty respect for the King of Israel. David would not touch the anointed King Saul, in spite of

convenient opportunity, even though Saul was intent upon killing
him.

> *1 Samuel 26:23 The Lord render to every man his
> righteousness and his faithfulness: for the Lord delivered thee
> into my hand to day, but I would not stretch forth mine hand
> against the Lord's anointed.*

- The Armourbearer of King Saul

When King Saul was surrounded in defeat, he did not desire
to be captured alive. When the King commanded a servant to kill
him in lieu of the fate of falling into the hands of the enemy, the
servant refused the order because of this partnership of *abah*.

> *1 Samuel 31:4 Then said Saul unto his armourbearer, Draw
> thy sword, and thrust me through therewith; lest these
> uncircumcised come and thrust me through, and abuse me. But
> his armourbearer would not; for he was sore afraid. Therefore
> Saul took a sword, and fell upon it.*

- Asahel and Abner

Asahel, one of the sons of Zeruiah, and a brother of Abishai
and Joab would not use wisdom when pursuing Abner, the
commander of the forces of Israel. The anointing of God was
upon Abner, and this mighty warrior warned Asahel to respect
the anointing. Asahel would not honor the issuance of *abah* upon
Abner, and came against Abner regardless of the warning. This
impetuous son of Zeruiah was killed.

> *2 Samuel 2:21 And Abner said to him, Turn thee aside to
> thy right hand or to thy left, and lay thee hold on one of the
> young men, and take thee his armour. But Asahel would not
> turn aside from following of him.*

The Search for an Heir

Abraham had a servant named Eliezer, and to this man was entrusted a duty of paramount importance. This servant was sent to find a wife for Isaac, the girl that would essentially become the matriarch of the line of covenant heritage. The choice had to be precise, being definitively ordered of God.

Many equate this selection process as being a type of the search for joint-heirs with Christ. This type of exploration is one being currently conducted by the Spirit of God. In reviewing the cited passage below, take note of the stringent direction Abraham gave to Eliezer. If a candidate for marriage would not display an *abah* to follow in a manner willing to disrupt her personal plan, do not accept her.

> *Genesis 24:4-5 But thou shalt go unto my country, and to my kindred, and take a wife unto my son Isaac. [5] And the servant said unto him, Peradventure the woman will not be willing to follow me unto this land: must I needs bring thy son again unto the land from whence thou camest?*

It is very clear Abraham was not prepared to go back into the place from which God had already caused him to leave. We must be very careful to follow what God has told us, and not be tempted to backtrack into familiar areas in an attempt to gratify a personal longing. God continually warns against looking back, turning back or desiring to go back. Unless, of course, the measure of repentance is applied to our own lives and we are returning to the pathway of God.

New Testament Abba

The most notable instances of *abah* are found in the New Testament. Each of the three illustrates a direct example of the concept of obedience in sonship. These examples of *abah* are all indicative of calling upon God on behalf of covenant responsibility.

The first of these is found in the life of our Lord Jesus, the firstborn of many brethren, and it took place in the Garden of Gethsemane prior to the trials preceding the Crucifixion.

> *Mark 14:36 And he said, Abba, Father, all things are possible unto thee; take away this cup from me: nevertheless not what I will, but what thou wilt.*

The Bible speaks of the night of prayer Jesus endured in the Garden of Gethsemane. The Gospel narratives are quite detailed concerning the anguish our Lord battled during these hours. The disciples were sleeping, and were seemingly unable to stay awake despite the pleas of our Lord encouraging them to intercede along with Him. Three times on this night the Lord made an appeal to the disciples, and each time He returned to His own prayer wherein He said the same words. What was the cry of our Lord? Abba, Father.

A total and complete commitment to the purpose of the Father was displayed here. A resolute devotion to the will of God is communicated. Some might wrongfully interpret these statements as being those of vacillation and fear, but nothing of the kind would ever have been spoken by Jesus.

Throughout His earthly life, He regularly commented He had come for the Cross. When Jesus willingly volunteered to come to earth to pay the price of redemption, He knew this was the ending sequence of the process. There is no variableness or shadow of turning with God, and there certainly would be none within this seminal moment of redemption.

When Jesus said "abba," He set the example for all following in the pathway of sonship. His entire life upon earth consisted of a continuing example of sonship. Jesus consistently spoke of doing the will of the Father or coming to the earth for the cause of the Father. This was the meaning of life for the Son of God. It must be our meaning, as well. When you became born again, the Spirit of sonship was accepted and taken by you. From that point you must cry "Abba, Father."

> **Romans 8:15** *For ye have not received the spirit of bondage again to fear; but ye have received the Spirit of adoption, whereby we cry, Abba, Father.*

In Galatians, the companion Epistle to the Book of Romans, we read the same sentiment. This time this spiritual motivation is not something we accept and take, as was the case in Romans 8. In Galatians we read since we are sons, God apostolically sends forth sonship to us. In this, we cry "Abba, Father."

> **Galatians 4:6** *And because ye are sons, God hath sent forth the Spirit of his Son into your hearts, crying, Abba, Father.*

The Spirit of God has created us for the purpose of partnering with the Heavenly Father. This is the sum total of our life as human beings. We must embrace His presence and begin to breathe His Spirit in full obedience to the plans and purposes of the Almighty.

The fulfillment of this pathway will be known by various demonstrations of the might and power of God. We will see the activation of the places upon the earth that have been waiting earnestly for the showing forth of the sons of God (Romans 8:19). This fulfillment of the creation of God will yield incredible signs and wonders in this hour. You have been born into the climactic moment of history. This is a time of vital import, as the scrolls of the end are being opened and unrolled according to the timetable of God.

What will you do in response to this information? How will you now react to what you have seen concerning your place before the Almighty? The heart of God is shown to you in a fresh manner, and this revelation is a gift from God to you. What you do with it now is between you and the Spirit of God. Will he find you willing and obedient?

Abba is not something we quietly hide within a corner. It does not allow for placid application within our life and ministry. *Abba* is something we cry out to achieve. It is like the calling of Samson, when the appeal for righteousness is loudly proclaimed. We are covenant children of the Most High. We must be bold in our identity, and in our appeal to the God who loves us.

The Breath of God and the Bride

At the end of the New Testament, a very powerful statement is made. In it, we find the essence of everything spoken in this book. What you are about to read from the Bible is the heart cry of God and of His people in this hour.

Revelation 22:17 And the Spirit and the bride say, Come. And let him that heareth say, Come. And let him that is athirst come. And whosoever will, let him take the water of life freely.

110

Come.

In this one word we feel volumes of expression and desire. The breath of God says come, and the people embodying His righteous intent say "Come." Those wanting His water of life as a mighty stream for this earth say "Come." Whoever desires to know God and drink deeply of Him must say "come."

The church has traditionally interpreted this epithet of the Book of Revelation as being a final word of appeal for the rapture of the church. In essence, "Come and get me God, I want out of here!" There is much work to do right here on earth on behalf of our covenant relationship with God. We say "come" as a point of loving devotion and commitment. Perhaps this is the mode of greeting Adam and the *ruwach* of God exchanged each day.

The Spirit of God and the bride say "come" to one another. They say "come" to a position of oneness. They say "come" to the point of partnership and to the place where God wants to dwell upon the earth. The voice of God and the voices of mankind join together to proclaim a desire vocalized since Eden: the wind of God and His people strongly desiring His presence upon the earth. This is the *abba* of God and His children.

Made in the USA
Middletown, DE
30 April 2019